K C Bowler, Kenway, G and G V Wilson

An Introduction to

OCCAM 2 Programming:

2nd Edition

WITHDRAWN
FROM
STOCK

Chartwell-Bratt

British Library Cataloguing in Publication Data
An introduction to occam 2 programming. - 2nd ed.
   1. Computer systems. Programming languages. Occam 2
   language
   I. Bowler, K. C. (Kenneth C.)
   005.13'3

ISBN 0-86238-227-0

© K C Bowler, R D Kenway, G S Pawley, D Roweth, G V Wilson and Chartwell-Bratt Ltd, 1989

Chartwell-Bratt (Publishing and Training) Ltd
ISBN 0-86238-227-0

Printed in Sweden,
Studentlitteratur, Lund
ISBN 91-44-27152-2

1 2 3 4 5 6 7 8 9 10 | 1993 92 91 90 89

Preface to Second Edition

The most significant change that we have made in the second edition is to include a new chapter on further examples, which deals in some detail with two substantial applications programs, written by Greg Wilson. It replaces a chapter which dealt with features of the Computing Surface that were rather specific to the Edinburgh environment and which we felt to be of limited value to the general reader. We decided to omit the short reference section on the occam 2 language on the grounds that more comprehensive descriptions are now widely available. We have also taken the opportunity to correct a number of errors and to add explanatory comments in some places. We are extremely grateful to all those readers who notified us of errors or made suggestions for improvements. However, the flavour of the book remains that of a working set of lecture notes, rather than a textbook, reflecting the origin of the project.

Ken Bowler and Richard Kenway,

Department of Physics
University of Edinburgh
February, 1989.

Preface to First Edition

This introduction to occam 2 was originally produced as a detailed set of
lecture notes for an intensive course, giving practical hands-on experience
in an emerging computer technology. As there is a real need for a publication in this field we have made some minor modifications to the notes to
satisfy a wider readership. Although the occam language is still in development we have chosen to present only that part of the putative language
that is actually implemented on our hardware, fully aware that later additions will be necessary. Our aim has therefore been to produce a low-cost
booklet for practical use. There are other publications concerning occam
2, notably that by Pountain, and these undoubtedly will contain the language constructs which are most likely to be included in future language
definitions.

The hardware on which all the examples have been tested is the Meiko
Computing Surface (CS), our version having 42 INMOS T414 transputers.
This has been supported by the Department of Trade and Industry and the
Computer Board, and was delivered in April 1986. Considerable progress
has been made during the last year by our Theory and Computational
Physics Group at Edinburgh, but it was thought not appropriate to include
much of this which is specific to the CS. Nevertheless we have included a
number of details of the Computing Surface.

Our lecture notes are understandably not in the usual format because
occam is not yet a language with a long history. It should be easy to read
through the first chapter and get an overall view of the language, but then
some further help is needed to use this information in practice. The final,
summary chapter, is designed for practical usage, giving cross-references
to the other chapters whenever fuller details are required. This chapter
contains a statement of the constructs of occam 2, but it also includes some
of the necessary information about OPS, the occam operating system, for
otherwise it would not be a full working tool.

The second chapter gives some simple programs ideal for the beginner,
and there is the added advantage that it is possible to implement these
programs on an IBM PC (with a B004 board). Chapter 3 follows with a
specific case study, showing how to use a number of processors on one prob-

lem. This is then followed by a chapter on the use of parallel algorithms; many problems have to be rethought in order to exploit the enormous possible gains that massive parallelism offers.

A chapter surveying some of the various parallel computers is intended to put the transputer and the Computing Surface in perspective. This leads on to a more thorough chapter on the Computing Surface itself, and although there are some details which are specific to our own version of the computer, the reader should get a good indication of the versatility of this MIMD computer.

The history of the development of the scientific computer owes much to the seemingly unreasonable demands of the physicist, but we do have a shrewd idea as to where the physical limitations on computer technology lie. To get yet another factor of a thousand it is clear to us that massive parallelism is the only way. We have been delighted to be able to discuss these matters with the designers in Meiko, and are especially indebted to Miles Chesney.

The last few years has been a very exciting time for us in Edinburgh. We started work on the ICL DAP in 1980, and this led to our acquisition of two DAPs, a growth of our commitment to large scale computation and a deepening of our understanding of the issues of parallelism. In all of this work, and in our future hopes, Professor David Wallace FRS has played a major and energetic role, for which we are all profoundly grateful. For my part I would like to take this opportunity to thank all my colleagues for such genuine and fruitful collaboration, especially to the other authors of this book who did by far the major part of the work.

Stuart Pawley, Professor of Computational Physics

Department of Physics
University of Edinburgh
April, 1987.

Contents

Chapter 1

Introduction to Occam 2

1.1 Some basic ideas

These lectures will provide an elementary introduction to concurrent programming using the occam language, which was developed by C.A. Hoare of Oxford University and D. May of INMOS Ltd. Although occam may be used on conventional computers, it has a special relationship with the INMOS Transputer, a high-performance VLSI microprocessor which was designed with on-chip communications to facilitate the construction of parallel processing systems of arbitrary size. Occam may be thought of as the assembly language of the transputer, although it can be regarded as a language in its own right.

Occam is based on the process model of computing. A process is an independent computation with its own program and data, which can communicate with other processes which are executing at the same time. A process can be thought of as a black box with inputs and outputs, that can communicate by message passing using explicitly defined channels. Processes can be connected together by such channels to build more complex concurrent systems. Each channel provides a one-way connection between two concurrent processes. Communication is synchronised; if a given channel is used for input in one process and output in a second process, communication takes place only when both processes are ready.

Occam enables a system to be described as a collection of concurrent processes which communicate with each other through channels. An occam program may be executed by an array of transputers. However, it is important to realise that the same program may be executed almost unchanged on a smaller array, or even on a single transputer. An occam channel describes communication in the abstract and does not depend upon a particular hardware implementation .

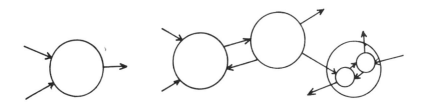

Figure 1.1: (a) A process (b) processes connected together by channels

ware implementation. Thus an occam program which uses channels may
be written and tested without deciding where particular processes will be
executed.

1.2   Primitive processes

Occam programs are constructed from a small number of simple building
blocks called primitive processes which we will now describe.

Assignment process

An assignment process simply changes the value of a variable, in just the
same way as in most other programming languages. The special symbol
used for assignment in occam is :=. Thus for example

```
var := 6
```

assigns the value 6 to the variable var. The value assigned to a variable
could be an expression, which may contain other variables:

```
var := 6 + var2
```

Note that = and := are not the same. In occam = means a test for equality,
not an assignment.

Input process

An input process inputs a value from a channel into a variable. The symbol for input in occam is ?. For example,

```
chan1 ? xvar
```

sets the variable xvar to the value input from the channel chan1. *Input processes can only input values to variables, not to constants or to expressions.* An input process will wait until a corresponding output process on the same channel is ready.

Output process

An output process outputs a value to a channel. The symbol for output in occam is !. Thus,

```
chan2 ! yvar
```

outputs the value of the variable yvar to the channel chan2. An output process cannot proceed until a corresponding input process on the same channel is ready.

Communication is thus synchronised; at any time a process may be ready and waiting to communicate on one or more of its channels. When both an input and an output process are ready to communicate on the same channel, the value to be output is copied from the output process to the input process.

SKIP and STOP

Occam also has two special processes called SKIP and STOP. SKIP is a process which starts, does nothing and then finishes. This may seem bizarre, but we will see later that there are instances where the syntax of occam requires a process to be present even though you want nothing to happen. It might also be used in a partially completed program to represent a process which has still to be written.

STOP is a process which starts but never proceeds or finishes ! You can think of it as representing a process which doesn't work. For example, it could be used instead of a process for handling errors, when a program is under development.

We should be more careful about what is meant by finishing. A process which completes all its actions is said to *terminate*. Normally a process starts, proceeds and terminates. A process which starts but cannot proceed is said to be *stopped*. A stopped process never terminates. For example, a process might be waiting for an input which will never happen because of a programming error; such a process is said to be *deadlocked*, the curse of concurrent programming !

1.3   Constructs

Constructs are used to combine primitive processes into larger processes which may, in their turn, be combined into larger processes still. Constructs start with an occam keyword which states how the component processes are to be combined.

SEQ

The sequential construct SEQ causes the component processes to be executed one after another, terminating when the last component terminates. For example

```
SEQ
    chan1 ? var1
    var2 := var1 + 1
    chan2 ! var2
```

which inputs from chan1 to var1, assigns var1 + 1 to var2 and outputs var2 to chan2. Thus we see that a SEQ process is just like a program in more conventional programming languages, terminating when the last component process terminates. *Note* that the component processes which make up the SEQ are all indented with respect to the word SEQ by two characters, which is how occam knows which processes are part of the SEQ construct. *Note* also that SEQ is compulsory in occam whenever two or more processes are to run in sequence, unlike more conventional languages, where the sequential execution of consecutive statements is usually taken for granted.

Replicated SEQ

Occam allows us to create replicas of processes using a replicator index akin to an array index. We shall postpone discussion of arrays until later, but here is an example of a replicated SEQ:

```
INT var :
SEQ index = 0 FOR 5
  channel.out ! var + index
```

The effect of this is equivalent to writing

```
INT var :
SEQ
  channel.out ! var
  channel.out ! var + 1
  channel.out ! var + 2
  channel.out ! var + 3
  channel.out ! var + 4
```

that is, we create 5 replicas of the input process and execute them in sequence. Another new feature is the declaration of the variable var to be of type INT, that is, integer. We will specify the types in occam a little later. The general form of a replicated SEQ is

```
SEQ index = base FOR count
  ... process
```

Note that the symbol ... is used to represent a *fold* in which part of the program which is not relevant to the example is hidden. It is not part of the syntax of occam. Individual processes in a replicated construct can be referred to using the replicator index. You will see examples very shortly. Note that if count is zero, the replicated SEQ will act like SKIP.

Naming a process

At this point it is useful to point out that a process may be named by means of the keyword PROC and a name, followed by the body of the process or procedure. PROC takes zero or more formal parameters, which will be described later. For example

```
PROC add.one (CHAN OF ANY chan1,chan2)
  INT var1, var2 :
  SEQ
    chan1 ? var1
    var2 := var1 + 1
    chan2 ! var2
:
```

Here we have packaged up the previous example code into a procedure named `add.one` which takes the names of the two channels `chan1` and `chan2` as parameters. The procedure is terminated by the : on a line by itself at the same level of indentation as the `PROC` keyword.

Scope

In occam, variables, channels and other named objects are local to the process which immediately follows their specification. Declarations, like `INT`, introduce variables for the process that follows at the *same level of indentation*. Indentation defines the scope of a construct.

WHILE

We may wish to have a process executed repeatedly, until some condition is satisfied. One way to achieve this is to use

> `WHILE` *expression*

which repeats the process within its scope until the boolean-valued *expression* evaluates to `FALSE`. This is the only way in which a `WHILE` loop can terminate. As a simple example consider an elementary buffer

```
WHILE TRUE
  INT xvar :
  SEQ
    buffer.in ? xvar
    buffer.out ! xvar
```

which repeatedly inputs a value from the channel `buffer.in` and then outputs it to channel `buffer.out`. The `SEQ` ensures that input is complete

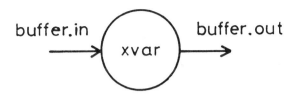

Figure 1.2: A simple buffer

before output starts. WHILE TRUE causes the whole sequential construct to be executed repeatedly, in this case without terminating, since *expression* is always TRUE.

We can easily package this as a procedure or named process:

```
PROC buffer (CHAN OF ANY buffer.in, buffer.out)
  WHILE TRUE
    INT xvar :
    SEQ
      buffer.in ? xvar
      buffer.out ! xvar
:
```

Such a procedure may then be attached to a following process by its terminating colon. We will give an example after introducing the next construct.

PAR

The parallel construct PAR causes the component processes to start execution simultaneously, terminating only after all the components have terminated. We illustrate its use by means of an example, a two-stage buffer which uses the PROC buffer just discussed

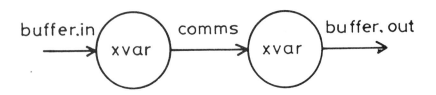

Figure 1.3: A two-stage buffer

```
CHAN OF ANY buffer.in, buffer.out, comms :
PAR
    buffer(buffer.in, comms)
    buffer(comms, buffer.out)
```

Here it is important to note that the written order of the component processes is irrelevant, as they are performed concurrently. Each process awaits
input on a channel and, upon receipt, outputs a value. In this example,
the concurrent processes communicate using the channel comms. In general
note the following:

- concurrent processes may only communicate using channels

- processes within a PAR construct must be independent

- each concurrent process operates on its own variables

- communication is synchronised.

- only two component processes of a PAR may use any particular channel, one as sender and the other as receiver.

Here is a second example, admittedly artificial, which does some arithmetic on the input values before passing them on:

```
CHAN OF ANY comms :
PAR
  INT var1 :
  SEQ
    channel.in ? var1
    comms ! var1*var1
  INT var2 :
  SEQ
    comms ? var2
    channel.out ! var2 + 1
```

We have here assumed that the channels `channel.in` and `channel.out` have been defined elsewhere in the program. Of course it would be much simpler in this instance to perform the square and add in a single `SEQ` process or in a single expression, but in more complicated applications, such as the construction of an arithmetic pipeline, this kind of construct can be very useful.

Replicated PAR

As for the `SEQ` construct, `PAR` may be replicated to build an array of parallel processes, any of which can be referred to by the replicator index. The general form is

```
PAR index = base FOR count
    ... process
```

As an example, we consider the 'bucket brigade' or pipeline, in which data is passed from one process to another in a chain, using an array, or vector of channels, which is declared in the first line. We will discuss arrays in detail at a later point, but the minimal use made here should be self-explanatory:

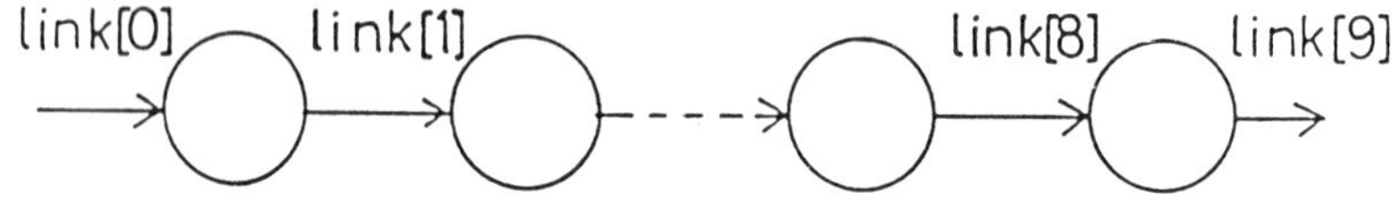

Figure 1.4: A pipeline of parallel processes

```
[10]CHAN OF ANY link :
PAR bucket = 0 FOR 9
   WHILE TRUE
     INT water :
     SEQ
       link[bucket] ? water
       link[bucket+1] ! water
```

The replicator sets up 9 parallel processes, each of which continually transfers values between one node in the pipeline and its neighbour. Of course
this example is not self-contained, because as it stands, the first 'bucket'
has nowhere to input its 'water' from, nor has the final process anywhere
to output its 'water' to. However, we can imagine embedding this code in
a larger program which supplies data to link[0] and extracts data from
link[9].

1.4   Operators

So far we have not specified the arithmetic and logical operators which are
available in occam. Let us now be more precise.

Arithmetic operators

The elementary arithmetic operations in occam are as follows:

```
a + b       -- add b to a
a - b       -- subtract b from a
a * b       -- multiply  a by b
a / b       -- divide a by b
a REM b     -- remainder when a is divided by b
a \ b       -- alternative form of REM
```

Note the use of occam comments, preceded by --.

In occam there is no priority for arithmetic operators so that brackets must be used to remove all ambiguities. For example:

```
(2+3)*(4+5)     -- result is 45
2+(3*(4+5))     -- result is 29
(2+(3*4))+5     -- result is 19
2+3*4+5         -- illegal
(2+(3*4)+5)     -- illegal
```

Modulo arithmetic operators

For integers only, a further set of operators is provided which permits modulo arithmetic. The modulo operators PLUS, MINUS and TIMES permit addition, subtraction and multiplication modulo N (=2 to the power n, where n is the number of bits in an INT), in unchecked 2's complement arithmetic. In general

(i PLUS j) is (i+j) + (k*N)

where k is the unique integer for which

(i+j) + (k*N) >= -(N/2) and (i+j) + (k*N) < (N/2)

Similarly

(i MINUS j) is (i-j) + (k*N)   (i TIMES j) is (i*j) + (k*N)

As a very simple example, consider the case of 3 bit INT modulo arithmetic, where N is 8:

(3 PLUS 3) is 6 ı k*N, with k = -1 and hence yields -2.

Boolean operators

A boolean value is produced as the result of a test performed by a comparison operator. The following operators are available in occam:

```
=        -- equal to
<>       -- not equal to
>        -- greater than
<        -- less than
>=       -- greater than or equal to
<=       -- less than or equal to
```

Note that again brackets are needed to remove ambiguities whenever more complicated tests are made by combining two or more comparisons.

Occam also provides the boolean constants TRUE and FALSE which may be used anywhere that a test could be used. We have already seen an example.

Occam provides the standard boolean operators AND, OR and NOT, which are defined by

```
NOT TRUE = FALSE        NOT FALSE = TRUE
TRUE AND log = log      FALSE AND log = FALSE
TRUE OR log = TRUE      FALSE OR log = log
```

where log is either TRUE or FALSE.

Bit operators

More sophisticated applications than those we have discussed so far may require operations on individual bits in a word. Occam provides the following bit operators:

```
/\       -- bitwise and
\/       -- bitwise or
><       -- bitwise exclusive or
~        -- bitwise not
<<       -- left shift
>>       -- right shift
```

Numeric constants can be entered in hexadecimal notation by preceding them with the # sign. For example,

```
#FE          -- equivalent to decimal 254
```

1.5 Types and specifications

Unlike the first version of occam, described in the Occam Programming Manual, published by Prentice Hall International in 1984, occam 2 requires that objects used by a program should have a type, which must be specified before using that object in a process. We have also been a little cavalier with names for variables and channels in the examples given so far, so let us now be more precise.

Names

Names must begin with a letter of the alphabet, may include letters, digits and the dot character and can be of any length. Upper and lower case are treated as distinct by occam. Occam keywords such as `SEQ`, `PAR`, `CHAN` and `PROC` are always in upper case and are reserved. Examples of valid names are:

```
x  X  var  var1  VarOne

var.one  very.long.name.for.variable
```

Data types

The types which are available for variables in occam are:

```
INT      -- an integer
BYTE     -- an integer in the range 0 to 255;
         -- can be used to represent characters
BOOL     -- logical; either TRUE or FALSE
```

Note that the wordlength for type `INT` is implementation dependent.

In addition to these generally available types, some implementations of occam permit some or all of the following types:

```
INT16     -- 16 bit integer
INT32     -- 32 bit integer
INT64     -- 64 bit integer
REAL32    -- 32 bit real
REAL64    -- 64 bit real
```

Type conversion

The use of typing in occam 2 is intended to prevent the use of values in inappropriate situations. Nevertheless there are occasions when it is convenient to convert one type to another in a program.

Let us suppose that number has been declared as INT but that digit is of type BYTE. We can add them together as follows:

```
number := number + (INT digit)
```

The reverse conversion, of INT to BYTE is of course only valid provided that the value is in the legal range for type BYTE, namely 0 to 255.

The conversions between type BOOL and types INT or BYTE are as follows:

INT TRUE or BYTE TRUE   is 1

INT FALSE or BYTE FALSE is 0

BOOL 1 is TRUE

BOOL 0 is FALSE

so that if the value of the boolean running is TRUE, then INT running is 1.

To convert between INT and REAL32, and *vice versa*:

REAL32 ROUND x converts x of type INT to type REAL32

INT ROUND x converts x of type REAL32 to type INT

REAL32 TRUNC x converts x of type INT to type REAL32

INT TRUNC x converts x of type REAL32 to type INT

Constants

In occam a name may be given to a constant value by using the specification

VAL *type name* IS *value* :

so you can write, for example

VAL INT hours IS 24, minutes IS 60 :

The type is normally omitted when it is obvious from the value. Possible ambiguities over BYTE and INT, or REAL32 and REAL64 are resolved by explicitly specifying the type of the value. Examples:

VAL empty IS 0 (BYTE) :

VAL pi IS 3.14159 (REAL32) :

The first of these is equivalent to VAL BYTE empty IS 0 :

The colon which ends a specification effectively joins that specification to the process which follows it, an idea which is emphasised by indenting the specifications to the same level as the process, as we noted earlier in our brief discussion of scope. Thus the scope of a specification is restricted to the following process. This is illustrated by the squarer/adder example which we discussed under PAR. The variables var1 and var2 are local to their respective SEQ processes.

Single characters may be written as the character enclosed by single quotes, for example, 'a'. Such a constant is treated as a single number of type BYTE in occam. Note that the integer ASCII code representing that character is INT 'a'

Continuations

When writing occam code we may sometimes create expressions or lists which occupy more than one line of text. There is no explicit way in occam of indicating that one line is a continuation of the previous line. However, the general rule is that in occam we may continue from one line to another at the same level of indentation, provided that the syntax makes it clear that a continuation is intended. In other words, a line which is to be continued

had better not terminate with a character which would allow the compiler
to suppose that the line is complete ! Examples:

```
very.long.variable.name := very.long.variable.name +
                           even.longer.variable.name
```

is fine, but

```
very.long.variable.name := very.long.variable.name
                           +even.longer.variable.name
```

is not.

Initialisation

In occam the value of a variable is unassigned until it has either input a
value or has been assigned a value. Furthermore, the value of a variable
has meaning only during the execution of the process for which it has been
declared. Once the process has terminated the variable no longer has a
well-defined value. If the process is to execute again you must ensure that
the variable has again been assigned a value. If you want a variable to keep
its value from one execution of a process to another, you can declare it in
an outer scope, that is, before a process which contains the process which
you wish to execute repeatedly.

Channels

The strong typing of constants, variables and expressions in occam 2 is
complemented by *channel protocols* which define and check that typing
is not violated by channel communication. Every channel has a protocol
associated with it when it is declared.

The most basic form is known as a *simple protocol* and consists of a
type. For example,

```
CHAN OF INT message:
CHAN OF REAL32 results:
```

There is one special type, ANY, which is used to define the so-called *anarchic protocol*. Thus a channel may be declared to be CHAN OF ANY, in which case the compiler will not check the communications for type violations. This is a language extension implemented in the present compiler to allow for communications with the outside world, where the protocol is unknown. *It is mandatory for the channels which correspond to hard links between transputers.*

Timers

A very useful feature of occam, especially for real-time applications, is the existence of objects of type TIMER, which behave like channels which can be input from, but not output to; the value input is the current time, of type INT, determined by the clock on the processor. For example,

```
TIMER clock :
INT time :
clock ? time
```

Typically, 1 tick of the clock is 64 microseconds. Whenever the value of time exceeds the maximum value that can be represented by an INT, it becomes maximum negative (2's complement) and continues counting towards zero (every 4.2 min in 16-bit, every 75 hr in 32-bit). Therefore *time differences must be calculated in modulo arithmetic.*

It is possible to declare more than one timer (although they will all return the same value when runnning on the same processor). Several components of a PAR *may input from the same timer.*

A *delayed input* is an input from a timer which cannot proceed until the time has reached a certain value. For example,

```
PROC delay (INT interval)
  TIMER clock :
  INT now :
  SEQ
    clock ? now
    clock ? AFTER now PLUS interval
:
```

Note: no variable changes value in a delayed input; the value from clock is only *compared* with the value of the expression now PLUS interval.

AFTER is a comparison operator which returns a boolean value:

x AFTER y is equivalent to (x MINUS y) > 0

Delayed input may be used in an ALT to provide a real-time wait. AFTER may be used to check whether one time is later than another, but *care must be taken* unless the difference between the two times is known to be less than the largest (2's complement) integer.

1.6 More on constructs

IF

Occam provides a form of conditional choice by means of the construct IF, which takes any number of processes, each preceded by a test, and builds from them a single process. The conditions are tested *sequentially* and the first one which is TRUE is executed. Note that *only* that process is executed. As an example, consider

```
IF
  var = 1
    chan1 ! x
  var = 2
    chan2 ! x
  var = 3
    chan3 ! x
```

The effect of this piece of code is to output the value of the variable x on chan1, chan2 or chan3 depending on whether the value of var is 1, 2 or 3. Note that if the value of var is anything other than 1, 2 or 3 the effect of this IF process is equivalent to STOP. The program can only proceed if one of the choices is executed. One way of avoiding this difficulty is as follows;

```
IF
  var = 1
    chan1 ! x
  var = 2
    chan2 ! x
  var = 3
    chan3 ! x
  TRUE
    SKIP
```

We see that if **var** fails the first three tests, it is bound to satisfy the fourth, namely TRUE, and hence the program can proceed via the SKIP process.

More complicated tests can be performed by nesting IF's:

```
IF
  var = 1
    chan1 ! x
  var = 2
    IF
      x = 6
        chan2 ! x
      TRUE
        chan3 ! x
  TRUE
    SKIP
```

If the value of **var** is 2 the effect of this code fragment is to output the value of x on chan3 if x has any value other than 6.

ALT

Whereas the IF construct enables us to choose different processes according to the values of variables in the program, the alternative construct, ALT, allows us to make choices which depend on the state of channels. The component parts of ALT, called *alternatives*, are combined by ALT into a single construct, but in ways which can be difficult to grasp at first. The simplest kind of ALT is where each alternative consists of an input process followed by an executable process of some sort. Thus

```
CHAN OF ANY chan1, chan2, chan3 :
INT var :
ALT
  chan1 ? var
    ... process 1
  chan2 ? var
    ... process 2
  chan3 ? var
    ... process 3
```

The `ALT` watches all the input processes, known as *guards*, and executes the process associated with the first input to become ready. We can think of the `ALT` construct as a first-past-the-post race between a set of channels, with only the winner's process being executed.

As a second example we consider again the simple buffer. `ALT` may be used to provide for an interrupt:

```
BOOL running :
SEQ
  running := TRUE
  WHILE running
    INT var, any :
    ALT
      buffer.in ? xvar
        buffer.out ! xvar
      interrupt ? any
        running := FALSE
```

Here the channel `interrupt` permits the termination of the continuous `WHILE` loop.

In general note the following features:

- each component process has a guard which is an input, with an optional condition. Permissible guards are:

    channel ? *variable*

    (*boolean*) & channel ? *variable*

    SKIP

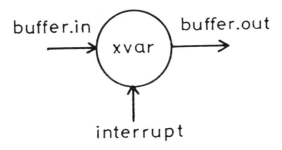

Figure 1.5: A simple buffer with interrupt

- a process which is guarded by an input is not executed unless the process at the other end of the channel is ready to output.

- the earliest process which is ready to be executed is chosen. The guard is executed, followed by the guarded process.

- if several alternative guards are ready, an arbitrary one is chosen.

- a process guarded by SKIP is always ready.

Here is an example of ALT with a test in addition to an input as guard:

```
CHAN OF ANY chan1, chan2, chan3 :
INT any :
ALT
   (ext.var < 0) & chan1 ? any
      ... process1
   (ext.var ~ 0) & chan2 ? any
      ... process2
   (ext.var > 0) & chan3 ? any
      ... process3
```

As with the IF construct, ALT may be nested inside an outer ALT.

1.7   A longer example

We now illustrate the use of these more difficult constructs with a longer
and somewhat more complex example. Suppose that we want to write a
program to control a heating system via two digital press-buttons labelled
warmer and cooler. Pressing warmer increases the heat output by one unit
whereas pressing cooler decreases the output by one unit.

Suppose that we have two occam channels called **warmer** and **cooler**
which produce an input whenever the appropriate button on the control
panel is pressed, and a third channel called **heater** whose function is to
transmit a value to the regulator mechanism on the heat source.

Without worrying about declarations at this stage, we first construct
simple processes to increase or decrease the heat produced:

```
SEQ
   heat := heat + 1
   heater ! heat
```

and

```
SEQ
   heat := heat - 1
   heater ! heat
```

The program can poll the two channels **warmer** and **cooler** to determine
which button has been pressed by making use of the **ALT** construct:

```
INT heat, any :
SEQ
  heat := 0
  heater ! heat
  WHILE TRUE
    ALT
      warmer ? any
        SEQ
          heat := heat + 1
          heater ! heat
      cooler ? any
        SEQ
          heat := heat - 1
          heater ! heat
```

The use of WHILE TRUE means that the control panel buttons are interrogated repeatedly and the process never terminates. We can ensure that the program terminates in a sensible fashion by adding an extra channel to communicate the status of the OFF button on the control panel to the program, and by replacing the boolean constant TRUE by a boolean variable which represents the ON/OFF status:

```
BOOL running :
INT heat, any :
SEQ
  running := TRUE
  heat := 0
  heater ! heat
  WHILE running
    ALT
      warmer ? any
        SEQ
          heat := heat + 1
          heater ! heat
      cooler ? any
        SEQ
          heat := heat - 1
          heater ! heat
      off ? any
        running := FALSE
```

We might also wish to limit the values which are transmitted to the heater
to some fixed range which corresponds with the physical limitations on the
minimum and maximum heat output of the device. Let us suppose that
these values are 0 and 10 respectively. We declare these minimum and
maximum values at the beginning of the program using named constants
so that if we ever need to revise the values, when, for instance a new model
of the heater is installed, we need only change the values in a single place
in the program.

```
VAL min.heat IS 0, max.heat IS 10 :
BOOL running :
INT heat, any :
SEQ
  running := TRUE
  heat := min.heat
  heater ! heat
  WHILE running
    ALT
      (heat < max.heat) & warmer ? any
        SEQ
          heat := heat + 1
          heater ! heat
      (heat > min.heat) & cooler ? any
        SEQ
          heat := heat - 1
          heater ! heat
      off ? any
        running := FALSE
```

Note that the channels heater, warmer, cooler and off have not been declared in the program because they connect to pieces of hardware, rather than to other occam processes.

1.8 Abbreviations

One of the most powerful and useful features of occam is the abbreviation. Abbreviations may be used to give a name to any expression in occam. We have already seen an example when we discussed named constants, employing VAL. Here is an expression abbreviation

```
VAL seconds IS 60*((60*hours)+mins) :
```

which defines seconds to be shorthand for the value of the expression on the right. The scope of the abbreviation is the process which follows it, to which it is attached by the terminating colon, as usual.

If an abbreviation, such as this example, contains variables on its right hand side, then in general those variables should remain constant throughout its scope. The full form of an expression abbreviation contains a type specifier before the name:

VAL *type name* IS *expression* :

but as before, the type can be omitted, leaving occam to deduce the type from the type of the right hand side. Occam assumes that integers less than 256 are of type INT unless otherwise instructed, which can be done:

    VAL soh IS 1 (BYTE) :

In the next section we shall see how abbreviations can be used to name arrays and parts of arrays.

1.9 Arrays

Unlike earlier versions of occam, occam 2 supports multidimensional arrays. Quite generally, an array is a set of elements of the same type. An array may have one or more subscripts; the number of subscripts is referred to as the dimension of the array. An element of an array is specified by giving the value of each of the array subscripts, and is usually known as a component of the array.

Array types

Array variables in occam are declared in the same way as single variables of any type, but with the number of components in each dimension prefixing the type declaration. Examples are:

```
[4]INT vector :            -- a vector of 4 integers

[8][8]BYTE chessboard :    -- a 2 dimensional byte array

[5][5][5]INT cube.sites :  -- a 3 dimensional integer array

[6]REAL32 values :         -- a vector of 6 reals

[3]CHAN OF ANY ttyMux :    -- a vector of 3 channels
```

An array can be referenced by name in order to transmit it to another process, for example.

```
PAR
   comms ! chessboard
   ... other processes
   comms ? chequer
```

sends the entire array `chessboard` to another process, provided that
`chequer` has also been declared to be of type `[8][8]BYTE`. Whole arrays
may also be assigned to and from.

Entire sub-arrays may also be accessed by specifying the appropriate
number of indices. For example, a 2-dimensional array may be referred to
either as a whole array, using its name, by 1-dimensional sub-arrays, using
a single subscript, or by elements, using two subscripts.

Note that the sizes of arrays in occam must be fixed at compile time and
cannot be assigned or altered during execution.

The convention for referring to particular components of arrays in occam is to specify the array name followed by a suffix or suffices giving the
particular values of the array subscripts in brackets. For example

```
vector[0]            -- the first element of vector

chessboard[0][1]     -- the white knight's square!

ttyMux[1]            -- the second channel
```

As an example, consider a process to output the values stored in a one-
dimensional array to a channel:

```
CHAN OF ANY chan.out :
[20]INT store :
SEQ
  component := 0
  WHILE component < 20
    SEQ
      chan.out ! store[component]
      component := component + 1
```

This could be done rather more elegantly using a replicator:

```
CHAN OF ANY chan.out :
[20]INT store :
SEQ component = 0 FOR 20
  chan.out ! store[component]
```

which illustrates the idea that a replicated SEQ is equivalent to a counted loop.

Arrays may be used as parameters to procedures. In occam, the size of an array parameter need not be declared when the PROC is specified, which allows the passing of an array of any size as an actual parameter, provided that it is of the correct data type. The type specifier for an array formal parameter looks like an array type with the size omitted. However, since a procedure may need to know the size of such an array, there is a special operator SIZE in occam which returns an INT value which is the size of the array. For example:

```
PROC read.in (CHAN OF ANY input, []INT vector)
  INT component :
  SEQ
    component := 0
    WHILE component < (SIZE vector)
      SEQ
        input ? vector[component]
        component := component + 1
  :
```

is a procedure which reads in values from a channel to a vector, and can legally be called with a 1-dimensional integer array of any size. In occam, multi-dimensional arrays are regarded as arrays of arrays. Thus the SIZE operator acting on a multi-dimensional array returns the number of sub-arrays existing at that level.

Array segments

An array segment consists of a set of consecutively numbered components of an array and is of the form

[*array* FROM *subscript* FOR *count*]

A segment can itself be treated as an array. Thus defining the array `[20]INT` `store` we may treat the segment

    [store FROM 8 FOR 6]

as an array of 6 components, starting with `store[8]` and ending with `store[13]`.

Array segments can be input, output or assigned to in the same manner as arrays, provided always that the expression which is assigned is an array of the same type and size as the segment. For example

    [store FROM 10 FOR 5] := [store FROM 0 FOR 5]

    [store FROM 10 FOR 5] := cache

where `cache` has been declared as `[5]INT`.

More about abbreviations

We have already met the use of abbreviations for constants and constant expressions. The description of array segments can be much simplified by using abbreviations. For example

    st IS [store FROM 10 FOR 5] :

enables us to consider `st` to be an array of size 5, with subscripts running from 0 to 4, where, for example, `st[1]` is identified with `store[11]` and so on.

An important point to note here is that `VAL` is not used; we are not merely naming a value. The abbreviation may thus be used instead of the full name of the object when we wish to change the value of that object by assignment or by input. We could write the previous example more succinctly as

    st := cache

Note that it is *not* legal, when using an abbreviation for an array component or segment, to change which component or components are referred to. For example, if we declare an abbreviation

    pocket IS store[i] :

we should not change the value of the subscript i within the scope of
pocket.

Abbreviations may also reward the programmer with performance ben-
efits, as well as improving the conciseness of code. If instead of subscripting
an array, we use an abbreviation for an array component within a loop

- the compiler recognises that the subscripts are constant and so does
  not compile run-time range checks

- the address of the array component becomes local to the loop process
  rather than global, and occam processes handle local data faster.

An abbreviation may also be used to set up an array constant:

```
VAL days IS [1,2,3,4,5,6,7] :
```

The components of days can be accessed in the usual way, so days[3] is 4.

RETYPES

Occam 2 provides a potentially powerful way of performing type conversion
in the form of an operator RETYPES whose use is of the general form

specifier name RETYPES *element*

or

VAL *specifier name* RETYPES *expression*

Warning: the use of retyping conversion will usually result in implementation dependent processes, as the representation of variables will vary from
one implementation to another.

RETYPES may be used to map arrays of different dimension on to one another. The example here shows how a three-dimensional array may be
retyped as a vector, or one-dimensional array.

```
VAL volume IS N*(N*N) :
[N][N][N]INT cube.sites :
[volume]INT vec.sites RETYPES cube.sites :
```

Tables

Tables are a means of generating an array value. Suppose that v is an INT variable, with current value 1. The table

```
[v, v+1, v+2]
```

generates an array of type [3]INT with component values 1, 2, 3. The array so generated may be referenced by subscript in the usual way:

```
[v, v+1, v+2][2]
```

or assigned to a variable:

```
INT v :
[3]INT vector :
SEQ
   ...
   vector := [v, v+1, v+2]
```

or abbreviated to a name for later use:

```
INT v, w :
...
VAL vector IS [v, v+1, v+2] :
SEQ
   ...
   w := vector[2]
```

Characters and strings

We have already seen that a single character may be represented in occam by a constant of type BYTE, for example 'a'. A text *string* may be written using double quotes, e.g. "Hello", and is treated by occam as an array of type [n]BYTE where n is the length of the string. The value of this sample string is equivalent to the value of the table ['H','e','l','l','o'].

Strings and character constants may contain any occam character (except *, ' and "). Certain special characters are represented as follows:

*c   carriage return

```
*n   newline
*t   horizontal tab
*s   space
*'   quote mark
*"   double quote
**   asterisk
```

Thus for example in sending a string to the VDU screen it is necessary to terminate the string with a carriage return/newline to flush the screen buffer by sending:

```
"Hello*c*n"
```

If a string contains the character pair *1 immediately after the opening ", the value of byte 0 of the string is the subscript of the last character of the string.

Any character can be represented by *# followed by two hexadecimal digits.

We finish this section on arrays with two examples to illustrate some of the features just introduced. Here is a procedure which can be used to compute the mean and variance of a set of data, as that data is accumulated.

```
PROC time.average ([]REAL32 statistics, REAL32 data)

  sample.size IS statistics[0] :
  sum.x IS statistics[1] :
  sum.x.sq IS statistics[2] :
  mean IS statistics[3] :
  variance IS statistics[4] :
  SEQ
    sample.size := sample.size + 1.0(REAL32)
    sum.x := sum.x + data
    sum.x.sq := sum.x.sq + (data*data)
    mean := sum.x/sample.size
    variance := (sum.x.sq/sample.size) - (mean*mean)
:
```

We see the use of an array as a formal parameter of a procedure, and abbreviations for array components. Note that in using this procedure, you must ensure that the actual array used when the procedure is called has been properly initialised. For instance

```
VAL zero IS 0.0(REAL32) :
VAL zero.stats IS [zero,zero,zero,zero,zero] :
REAL32 pulse.height :
[5]REAL32 pulse.height.stats :
SEQ
  --initialisation
  pulse.height.stats := zero.stats
  WHILE TRUE
    SEQ
      -- read event and update statistics
      data.chan ? pulse.height
      time.average (pulse.height.stats, pulse.height)
```

In the second example we use a formal parameter which is an array of constants, rather than variables, in a procedure which computes the scalar product of two fixed vectors:

```
PROC scalar.product (VAL []REAL32 a, b, REAL32 a.b)
  SEQ
    a.b := 0.0 (REAL32)
    SEQ i = 0 FOR (SIZE a)
      a.b := a.b + (a[i]*b[i])
  :
```

Here a.b is initialised to zero and then used to accumulate the products of the corresponding components of the vectors a and b.

1.10 More on replicators

We saw earlier that replicators could be used with the SEQ and PAR constructs to useful effect. Now that we are armed with more details of the properties of arrays in occam we could proceed to construct more complex examples of their use, but instead we will introduce two more kinds of replicated construct, IF and ALT.

Replicated IF

The general form is

```
IF index = base FOR count
   choice
```

where *choice* consists of a condition followed by a process. Here is a very simple example:

```
IF component = 0 FOR 5
   store[component] = 0
     store[component] := 1
```

whose effect is simply to test the first 5 elements of the array store and to replace the first one found to be 0 by 1. Note, however, that if no 0 is found, the program will be stopped. The replicated construct does not admit (sensibly) a concluding TRUE SKIP, and hence the usual use of a replicated IF involves nesting within an outer IF. For instance

```
IF
   IF component = 0 FOR 5
     store[component] = 0
       store[component] := 1
   TRUE
     SKIP
```

will now SKIP if no zeroes are found in the array, and the program can proceed. This construct can be used for searching for the first occurrence of a given character in a string. If all such occurrences are needed a replicated SEQ may be used instead.

Replicated ALT

The general form of the replicated ALT is similar to the previous construct:

```
ALT index = base FOR count
   alternative
```

where *alternative* is a guard followed by a process. The effect is to monitor an array of channels and it may therefore be used to construct a multiplexer, for example:

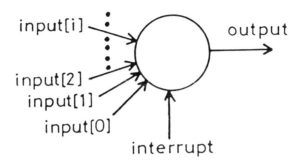

Figure 1.6: A multiplexer

```
PROC mux([]CHAN OF ANY input,
         CHAN OF ANY output, interrupt)

  INT any, signal :
  BOOL running :
  SEQ
    running := TRUE
    WHILE running
      ALT
        ALT i = 0 FOR (SIZE input)
          input[i] ? signal
            output ! signal
        interrupt ? any
          running := FALSE
  :
```

1.11 Priority

It is sometimes useful, particularly in real-time programming, to be able to assign priorities to processes in a well-defined way. We saw earlier in the case of the ALT construct that when the inputs guarding two alternative processes become ready simultaneously, occam makes an arbitrary choice between the two. Occam allows us to assign priorities for the ALT and the

PAR constructs by preceding the keyword by PRI. In either case the component processes are assigned a priority which corresponds to the textual order in which they appear in the program.

PRI ALT

As already indicated, when two processes become ready simultaneously, the process with the higher priority will be executed. An example of the use of this construct is when it is essential to guarantee that a particularly important channel is examined:

```
WHILE running
  INT any :
  PRI ALT
    emergency.halt ? any
      running := FALSE
    TRUE & SKIP
      ... main cycle
```

Here the PRI ALT forces the program to check the channel emergency.halt because of its higher priority. Without the priority, the alternative TRUE & SKIP, which is always ready, could be taken at every cycle of the WHILE loop.

PRI PAR

Assigning priorities to the component processes means that processes with lower priority can proceed only if no higher priority process is able to proceed. Consider

```
PRI PAR
  SEQ
    chan1.in ? var1
    chan1.out ! var1
  SEQ
    chan2.in ? var2
    chan2.out ! var2
```

where the second SEQ cannot proceed, even when ready, unless the first is waiting for its input or output.

As an example, it might be the case that it is more important to relay any messages to an external device than to continue computation in a program. PRI PAR can be used to ensure that computation only proceeds when there is no message waiting to be input or output:

```
PRI PAR
  WHILE TRUE
    [message.length]BYTE message :
    SEQ
      message.in ? message
      SEQ i = 0 FOR message.length
        message.out ! message[i]
  ... main computation
```

We have assumed for illustrative purposes that the external device on the other end of channel message.out requires serving with data one byte at a time.

When running a high priority process of this kind it is generally a good rule to buffer the communications to other processes so that data can be sent without delay. The size of buffer needed depends in practice on the timings of the various processes involved.

```
PRI PAR
  CHAN OF ANY buffer.chan :
  PAR
    WHILE TRUE
      [message.length]BYTE message :
      SEQ
        message.in ? message
        buffer.chan ! message
    WHILE TRUE
      [message.length]BYTE message :
      SEQ
        buffer.chan ? message
        SEQ i =0 FOR message.length
          message.out ! message[i]
  ... main computation
```

As a general rule, `PRI PAR` should only be used when it is essential to impose explicit priority. Since priority does not impinge upon the logical structure of a program, it is really a configuration issue rather than an occam programming issue and thus should be left until last, when the overall program logic has been established and the program works.

1.12   More on procedures

We have already seen several examples of procedures and their uses in earlier sections, but we have not discussed in a systematic way the rules for their use or the conventions for parameter passing. Let us now remedy this deficiency.

Scope

Procedures obey the same scope rules as other occam objects such as names and variables; the procedure is only known throughout the process which immediately follows it, to which it is linked by the final `:`. The body of the `PROC` is executed whenever its name is found in that process; such an occurrence of the name is called an *instance* of the procedure. Whenever an instance of the `PROC` is encountered, it is executed exactly as if the body of the procedure had been substituted for the name.

Parameters

Earlier examples of `PROC`s introduced the idea of *formal parameters* which are the means by which different values may be passed to and from the body of the procedure at different instances. Formal parameters may be of any type, including, as we have seen, `CHAN`. When the body of the `PROC` is substituted for the instance of the procedure name in a process, the formal parameter names are replaced by the actual parameters, which may be values, variables or expressions.

We are allowed by occam to have any number of formal parameters, which must be separated by commas in the heading of the `PROC` definition. The actual parameters of an instance are similarly separated by commas, and must correspond in number, position and type with the formal parameters of the `PROC`.

Passing conventions

When we pass a variable as an actual parameter *to* a procedure in occam, that variable effectively replaces the formal parameter throughout the procedure. Anything which the procedure does to the formal parameter is also done to the variable, which may in consequence have its value changed. This is in *contrast* to the call-by-value convention commonly used in other programming languages in which the actual parameter is used as the initial value of the formal parameter, which then behaves as a local variable of the procedure. To give a very simple example, consider the procedure :

```
PROC double (INT number)
  number := 2 * number
:
```

When an instance of this procedure is encountered, such as double (n), the value of n will be twice its previous value when double (n) terminates, so that caution may be required. For example

```
INT n, m :
SEQ
  n := 1
  m := 2
  double (n)
  m := m + n
```

assigns a final value of 4, not 3, to m.

We sometimes require that a procedure should not alter the value of a variable which has been passed to it as a parameter. One way to achieve this is of course to assign the value of the parameter to a local variable within the PROC and to perform any operations on this local copy. If we need only the original value of a variable in the body of a procedure, that is, the formal parameter is never altered by assignment or by input, then we can say explicitly that only the value is to be passed, using VAL. We saw an example of this in the code for the scalar product of two vectors, given earlier. In this case, the formal parameter can be thought of as a constant throughout the body of the procedure. The compiler may exploit this to produce more efficient code.

We rewrite the heating system controller program to exploit the properties of procedures and to illustrate some of these points:

```
VAL more IS 1, less IS -1 :
BOOL running :
INT heat, any :
PROC alter.temp (VAL INT step)
  SEQ
    heat := heat + step
    heater ! heat
:
SEQ
  heat := 0
  heater ! heat
  running := TRUE
  WHILE running
    ALT
      warmer ? any
        alter.temp (more)
      cooler ? any
        alter.temp (less)
      off ? any
        running := FALSE
```

Note that the body of the PROC uses the variable heat even though it is not declared anywhere within the procedure, either as a local variable or as a formal parameter. heat is called a *free* variable with respect to the PROC alter.temp. Most importantly, it retains its value from one call of the procedure to the next, which is why we use it here. Of course, heat must be declared somewhere *before* the PROC definition. In general, a variable is *free* with respect to a procedure when the procedure is defined *within* the scope of that variable.

1.13   More on channel protocols

We saw earlier that every channel has a protocol associated with it when it is declared. The general form is

CHAN OF *protocol*

and we saw examples of simple protocols.

Sequential protocols

Sequential protocols are a means by which several items of different type
may be transmitted along a single channel. The types are separated by
semi-colons in the protocol definition, and the order in which they appear
specifies the order in which they must be used. For example

```
CHAN OF INT;INT;REAL32 comms :
INT first.int, second.int :
REAL32 float :
PAR
  comms ! 15; 42; 3.14159(REAL32)
  comms ? first.int; second.int; float
```

The PROTOCOL keyword

Protocols can be defined on their own for later use in channel definitions
by means of the occam keyword PROTOCOL. For instance,

```
PROTOCOL two.int IS INT;INT :
CHAN OF two.int chan1, chan2, chan3 :
```

declares a protocol in which all messages consist of two integers and then
declares three channels of that type. Another very useful example is a
protocol for transmitting arrays, in which each message consists of a size,
followed by an array:

```
PROTOCOL array.prot INT::[]INT :
```

which could be used to implement a more elaborate version of the simple
buffer process described earlier;

```
PROC buffer (CHAN OF array.prot in, out)

  INT array.size :
  [buffer.size]INT array :
  WHILE TRUE
    SEQ
      in ? array.size::array
      out ! array.size::array
:
```

1.14 Functions

A function is a special kind of named process which returns a result. Occam
functions have the virtue that, because of the strict rules about how they are
constructed, they are free of unpleasant side effects elsewhere in a program.
As an example, consider a function which compares two integers and returns
the value of the larger:

```
INT FUNCTION larger(VAL INT a, b)
  INT answer :
  VALOF
    SEQ
      IF
        a > b
          answer := a
        a < b
          answer := b
        a = b
          answer := a    -- could equally well choose b
    RESULT answer
:
```

Notice that a type specifier precedes the keyword FUNCTION, indicating the
type of the value returned by the function. Functions can appear wherever
an expression would appear. For example;

```
                winner := larger(a, b)
```

More generally, functions take the form

```
type FUNCTION name(parameter list)
 specification  :
  VALOF
    process
    RESULT expression
```

The following rules must be observed:

- formal parameters can only be VAL parameters

- PAR and ALT constructs cannot be used within the function

- input and output cannot be used within the function

- only variables defined within the scope of the function can be assigned to

- *free* variables can be read from, but not assigned to

1.15   Postscript

In these lectures we have tried to give an overview of the occam programming language in enough detail, and with sufficient examples, to enable you to start writing your own occam programs. No attempt has been made to be comprehensive or definitive; for this you must refer to the INMOS product definition for occam 2, which describes features that have not been covered in these lectures and, in some instances, have not yet been implemented in the currently available compiler releases. Highly recommended also is the INMOS document 'A Tutorial Introduction to Occam Programming', written by Dick Pountain and David May, which was an invaluable aid in the preparation of these lectures and the source of many useful examples.

Chapter 2

Implementation of Simple Programs

2.1   The Occam Programming System

The Occam Programming System, OPS, is an environment provided by
Meiko from within which programs can be written, compiled and run. OPS
runs on the Meiko Computing Surface and also on PC-based workstations.
A similar system, TDS, is available from Inmos.

Occam allows the user to develop a hierarchy of processes that reflects
the structure of the application, and OPS allows a hierarchical representation of an occam program via a mechanism known as *folding*. Folding is
analogous to taking a document with headed paragraphs and then folding
it so that the text is hidden, leaving only the headings visible, as illustrated
in figure 2.1.

Folds can be opened to reveal, in context, their contents, or closed,
leaving only the header visible. Folds can also be *entered*, in which case
only the contents of that fold are displayed, not the surrounding context.
Folds can be nested to any depth.

It should be noted that the editor marks closed folds by ... followed
by the fold header. The start of an open fold is marked by {{{ and the
header, and the end by }}} on a line of its own.

There are two approaches to the use of folds:

- **Procedural:** having written a procedure it can be checked, docu-
mented and then folded away, represented only by its header. This
approach is suitable for a library of procedures.

49

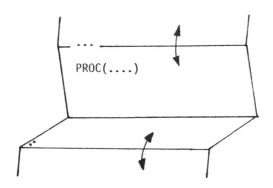

Figure 2.1: Folding up text

- **Top-down programming:** the folding editor encourages top-down development of code. A high-level program description can be written using occam constructs and folds (which may be empty) representing distinct tasks and their inter-relationships, for example:

```
{{{ test application

PROC job(CHAN OF ANY in, out, VAL INT const)

  ...   system code
  ...   libraries
  ...   declaration of variables
  SEQ
    ...   initialisation
    WHILE running
      SEQ
        ...   task 1
        PAR
          ...   task 2
          ...   task 3
        ...   task 4
    ...   termination
  :
}}}
```

At this stage the user can decide upon the channels needed for communication between processes running concurrently. Having written this specification, the details of each of the tasks can be filled in in the same way, representing the structure of each task in terms of constructs and subtasks. This process is repeated down to the lowest level of elementary processes and library procedures.

2.1.1 Files and folds

Files are created within OPS by folding up text and *filing* the fold. This creates a file whose name is the first word on the fold header, with .tsr as the default extension. OPS attaches a prefix F to the fold header to denote a filed fold.

Existing files can be attached to folds. To do this, an empty fold is created, the filename is typed on the fold header and the fold is filed. The message `File attached to fold` appears when the process is complete. If the contents of an existing file are to be used as the basis for a new file then the old file should be attached to an empty fold, unfiled, the name changed on the header, and then refiled.

The various operations of creating, opening, closing and filing folds, and so on, correspond to special sequences of keystrokes.

OPS makes extensive use of folding:

- on starting up OPS, a toplevel fold called `toplevel.top` is entered, from which all work is accessed

- all help information and utility parameters are held in folds

- most importantly, folds have attributes associated with them. A fold is designated `SC` if it contains procedures for separate compilation, `PROGRAM` if it contains compiled procedure definitions and placement information, `EXE` if it contains procedures suitable for running from within OPS, or `COMMENT` if its contents are to be ignored by the compiler.

2.2 Configuration

Configuration is what happens at the topmost level of an occam program to determine *how the program is mounted on particular hardware*. Configuration associates specific processes with real processors, and specific occam channels with real hard links. *It does not affect the logical behaviour of the program.*

There are two distinct types of occam program:

- an EXE which runs on the same transputer as OPS;

- a PROGRAM which runs on different transputers from OPS.

These are introduced in the next two sections; only as much detail as is required to implement simple programs is given. Most systems offer more I/O facilities than are used here (e.g. reading and writing files!) and a full description should be sought in the system manual.

2.3   EXEs

An EXE is an occam program which runs on the same transputer as OPS. It is therefore the only choice on a single-transputer workstation. It may also be the better choice on a multi-transputer machine at early stages in the development of a program, because it simplifies the configuration. As we shall see in the next section it is relatively straightforward to convert an EXE into a PROGRAM.

In the simplest type of EXE the complete program is packaged as an occam procedure with the channels from.ops and to.ops as formal parameters. The fold containing this procedure is filed and labelled EXE. It may then be compiled, linked and run, inputting from the keyboard and outputting to the terminal screen.

2.3.1   Hello World

Traditionally, the most elementary program is one which writes hello on the terminal screen. An EXE which does this is

```
{{{  EXE hello.tsr
{{{F hello.tsr
PROC hello (CHAN OF ANY from.ops, to.ops)
  #USE "/syslib/streams/streams.lib"
  ...  PROC filter
  CHAN OF ANY screen:
  PAR
    filter(screen, to.ops)
    INT any:
    SEQ
      Writes(screen, "hello*C*N")
      from.ops ? any
      screen ! endstreamch
:
}}}
...F hello.dcd code
...F hello.dds descriptor
...F hello.dlk link
...F hello.ddb debug
...F hello.ce1 CODE EXE hello.tsr
}}}
```

It is worth analysing the structure of this program in some detail and we proceed from the top down.

1. Inside the EXE fold is a fold containing the occam source code (with file extension .tsr) and five other filed folds which contain compiled code and other system information generated by the compiler.

2. The channels from.ops and to.ops are formal parameters and, as such, may have any name. However, the system assumes that the first channel in the list is for input from the keyboard and that the second channel is for output to the terminal screen.

3. #USE "/syslib/streams/streams.lib" is a reference to the library which contains I/O procedures, which are then available everywhere within the scope of the #USE statement. One of these procedures is Writes which outputs a string of characters to a channel. Its definition is

```
PROC Writes (CHAN OF ANY out, VAL []BYTE string)
  SEQ i = 0 FOR SIZE string
    out ! INT string[i]
  :
```

This sends the characters in the BYTE array string sequentially down the channel out. SIZE string gives the number of elements in the array string. The particular *instance* of Writes in hello replaces the *formal parameter* out by the *actual parameter* screen, and similarly replaces string by "hello*C*N". Notice that the 'newline' (*N) and 'carriage return' (*C) characters must follow the text of the message. This is because the to.ops channel is buffered, and otherwise would not display the message until the buffer is full. The effect is to write hello on the terminal screen and place the cursor at the start of a new line.

4. The closed fold ... PROC filter contains the definition of the *system procedure* filter. It acts as an interface between the user process and the terminal screen, running in parallel with the user process, implementing a particular *communications protocol*. Opening the fold,

```
PROC filter (CHAN OF ANY in, to.ops)
  VAL tt.out.int IS BYTE 19:
  INT char:
  SEQ
    in ? char
    WHILE char <> endstreamch
      SEQ
        to.ops ! tt.out.int; char
        in ? char
  :
```

we see that its action is to precede every integer sent to the channel to.ops by the *flag* tt.out.int, which tells OPS to expect an integer en route to the terminal screen. This protocol is not required within PROGRAMs. The reason for explicitly introducing the filter process, rather than incorporating it into the streams library procedures, is twofold:

(a) it permits the same streams library to be used in both EXEs and PROGRAMs hence simplifying the conversion from one to another;

(b) it provides the simplest illustration of how *system procedures* are incorporated in a program. [1]

Note that if several values are to be output to the same channel sequentially, this may be written as a single line of occam in which the values are separated by semicolons, i.e. the output in `filter` is equivalent to

```
SEQ
  to.ops ! tt.out.int
  to.ops ! char
```

5. The last of the declarations in `hello` is the channel `screen` which is used for internal *plumbing* between the user process and the system code.

6. The active part of the occam begins with the PAR statement which runs the system code in *parallel* with the user process.

7. The user process is the SEQ construct containing three component processes. The first is an instance of `Writes` which carries out the desired output. The other two component processes are concerned with *graceful* termination of the EXE.

   `from.ops ? any` prevents the EXE from terminating (and returning to OPS) before the user has a chance to read the message; it holds up the program until the user hits a key.

   `screen ! endstreamch` sends a predefined (in the streams library) value to the `filter` process to terminate it. The EXE cannot terminate until both of the component processes in the PAR have terminated; it is the user's responsibility to terminate his part of the program *and* the system code.

2.3.2 ASCII Codes

Now for a program that does something useful. Omitting the EXE foldset, this is

---

[1] More complex system code is contained in libraries, obviating the need for recompilation every time a user's program is changed.

```
{{{F ascii.tsr
PROC ascii (CHAN OF ANY from.ops, to.ops)
  #USE "/syslib/streams/streams.lib"
  ... PROC filter
  CHAN OF ANY screen:
  PAR
    filter(screen, to.ops)
    INT char :
    SEQ
      Writes(screen, "Hello *C*N")
      char := 0
      WHILE char <> 32
        SEQ
          from.ops ? char
          screen ! char; 32
          Writen(screen, char)
          Writes(screen, "*C*N")
      screen ! endstreamch
  :
}}}
```

and it has the following additional features.

1. The structure is much the same as hello; only the user process is changed. This repeatedly inputs a value for char from the keyboard, does a sequence of outputs to the terminal screen and terminates, after closing down filter, when char takes the value 32.

2. from.ops ? char inputs the code for a single character typed at the keyboard into the variable char. This is usually the *ASCII code* for the key typed, so that if the 1 key is pressed char receives the value **49**, which is the ASCII code for the numeral 1. The same applies in sending characters to the terminal screen; sending **49** will result in a 1 appearing on the screen. In occam 'x' is the ASCII code for the character x and is of type BYTE.

3. The program ascii outputs the ASCII code for any key that is pressed, terminating when it receives the ASCII code for 'spacebar' (32). Outputting a number to the screen is performed by the procedure Writen (CHAN OF ANY out, VAL INT n), which is too long to describe here. It has the effect of outputting the ASCII codes for

successive digits of the integer n to the channel out, each preceded by the appropriate protocol.

4. If it is required to do arithmetic with the numbers input from the keyboard, they have to be adjusted by subtracting 48 or INT '0'. Similarly, adding INT '0' converts a number of type INT to its ASCII code of type INT.

2.4 PROGRAMs for One Transputer

As the next step towards parallel processing consider two transputers, one running OPS and the other running a user program. The degree of parallelism in the implementation of the user program is unchanged from a EXE, however the configuration is quite different.

As a matter of terminology, we will call

host the transputer running OPS;

master the transputer directly connected to the host which handles I/O with the outside world (terminal, files on disk, etc.) and which may control a number of slave transputers;

slave any other worker transputer which is usually part of the main computational resource.

Thus, in this section we consider just a host and a master. We assume that the PROGRAM is booted from within OPS (for *standalone* PROGRAMs it is necessary to refer to the system manual). Then *no part* of the user program resides on the host i.e. the host runs only system code.

2.4.1 Configuration

The toplevel of such a PROGRAM for a pair of transputers within a Computing Surface domain comprises a *separately compilable* (SC) module for the master, which contains the user program, together with configuration information. The general structure is

```
{{{  PROGRAM one_transputer.tsr
{{{F one_transputer.tsr
...  SC master.tsr
...  Meiko board types
VAL board IS MK04X:
VAL hostlink IS 2:
PROCESSOR 1 T8
  master(board, hostlink)
}}}
...F code
...F descriptor
...F CODE PROGRAM one_transputer.tsr
}}}
```

and the various features are described below.

1. The PROGRAM foldset contains four filed folds. The first contains the
   source code and is open in the above example, the remainder contain information generated by the configurer and the load module
   produced by the extractor.

2. The toplevel of the source code contains the definition of the process
   that is to run on the master transputer, here also called master. This
   must be separately compilable i.e. have no external references except
   through its formal parameter list.

3. There follows a sequence of declarations and an instance of the process master. The declarations assign values to parameters required by
   master. Here these are the type of Meiko board on which the process
   master is to run (the fold ... Meiko board types contains definitions of the board names, such as MK04X), and the number of the link
   on the master transputer which is connected to the host transputer
   (link 2 in this example). Note that if the domain is hard-wired it
   will be necessary to find out from the system manager how the transputers are connected; if the domain is electronically configurable the
   choice is free.

4. The instance of the process master is preceded by *placement information* in the form of a PROCESSOR statement. This specifies the type
   of transputer on which master is to run (T2, T4 or T8) and assigns
   to it an arbitrary identifier (here 1) which may be used inside the
   program.

2.4.2   Master Template

The next level in the fold structure of the PROGRAM one_transputer is
the SC master.tsr. Opening this fold reveals five filed folds, the first,
master.tsr, contains the occam source and the others information generated by the compiler. The occam source code is rather different in detail
from that for an EXE although the structure is similar:

```
{{{F master.tsr
PROC master(VAL INT board, hostlink)
   ...   system libraries
   ...   PROC user.process
   {{{  channel declarations
   CHAN OF ANY keyboard, screen, debug, mouse:
   [4]CHAN OF ANY from.filer, to.filer:
   }}}
   PAR
     masterSys(keyboard, screen, debug, mouse,
               from.filer, to.filer, board, hostlink)
     user.process(keyboard, screen, debug)
   :
}}}
```

Thus, the system process masterSys, which is defined in one of the system
libraries, plays a role similar to filter in an EXE. It provides the user
process with access to a range of I/O facilities via the host transputer.
In this example we only make use of the channels keyboard and screen
which route messages from the terminal keyboard and to the terminal screen
respectively, and debug which provides a route to the Meiko supervisor bus.

2.4.3   A Benchmark Program

As a further example of a simple occam program, user.process might be
replaced by flops in the master template and the fold ... PROC
user.process by

```
{{{F flops.tsr
PROC flops (CHAN OF ANY keyboard, screen, debug)
  ... find.machine.type
  ... multiplies
  INT any, num, ticks.per.sec :
  SEQ
    find.machine.type(ticks.per.sec)
    ... output machine type
    ... input number of operations
    multiplies(num, ticks.per.sec)
:
}}}
```

This program computes the number of multiplications performed per second
by a transputer. It does this by first determining the clock rate of the
transputer, then counting the number of ticks of the clock between starting
and ending some number of operations supplied by the user, and finally
converting this into flops. The PROGRAM could equally well be an EXE,
differences are alluded to in the following analysis.

1. The references to system code occur in the master template; flops
   is within the scope of these, so that no further references are needed
   and, in particular, I/O utilities such as Writes are available.

2. There is no filter process; this has been replaced by masterSys at
   a higher level.

3. find.machine.type is a process which measures the number of ticks
   per second of the clock on the transputer being used. It is defined in
   the fold ... find.machine.type as:

```
{{{ find.machine.type
PROC find.machine.type (INT ticks.per.sec)
  TIMER time :
  INT start, end:
  SEQ
    time ? start
    SEQ i = 0 FOR 5
      SKIP
    time ? end
    end := end MINUS start
    IF
      end <= 1
        ticks.per.sec := 15625
      TRUE
        ticks.per.sec := 625000
  :
}}}
```

This times the operation SKIP and, on the basis of the number of ticks, determines which of the two possible clock speeds the transputer has.

4. The code for outputting the machine type and inputting the number of operations is contained in the following two folds:

```
{{{ output machine type
Writen(screen, ticks.per.sec)
Writes(screen, " ticks per sec*C*N")
}}}
{{{ input number of operations
Writes(screen, "How many operations ?*C*N")
Readn(keyboard, num)
}}}
```

The utilities for writing to the screen were described in section 2.3.1 and section 2.3.2. Readn is similar, except that it reads an integer, num, from keyboard and echoes it to the screen.

5. multiplies times the chosen number of multiplications.

```
{{{ multiplies
PROC multiplies (VAL INT num, ticks.per.sec)
  INT start, end, ticks :
  REAL32 a, b, c, flops :
  TIMER clock :
  SEQ
    b := 1.2345(REAL32)
    c := 0.9876(REAL32)
    clock ? start
    SEQ i = 0 FOR num
      a := b * c
    clock ? end
    ticks := end MINUS start
    flops :=((REAL32 ROUND ticks.per.sec) *
            (REAL32 ROUND num))/(REAL32 ROUND ticks)
    Writen(screen, INT ROUND flops)
    Writes(screen, " flops for multiplication*N*C")
  :
}}}
```

The new features of this PROC are the assignment of REAL32 values
to b and c and the *type conversion* required in the computation of
flops to avoid integer overflow. REAL32 ROUND x converts x of type
INT to type REAL32 and INT ROUND converts back again (rounding and
applying IEEE standards). Note the use of parentheses to specify the
order of the arithmetic operations; occam insists on this.

6. Finally, there is no need to terminate the process master gracefully,
   since leaving it in a bad state does not hang OPS which is running
   on a different transputer.

A good exercise, relating to the optimisation of occam programs, is to *un-
roll* the replicated SEQ around the multiplication, i.e. replace it by multiple
copies of the statement a := b * c.

2.5   PROGRAMs for More Than One Transputer

2.5.1   Configuration

A PROGRAM for more than one transputer requires a slight extension of the
configuration information in the example above. This is illustrated in the

following example for a ring of five transputers. A schematic diagram of
the PROGRAM is shown in figure 2.2.

```
{{{   PROGRAM multi_transputer.tsr
{{{F multi_transputer.tsr
...   SC master.tsr
...   SC slave.tsr
{{{   declarations
...   Meiko board types
...   link definitions
VAL master.board IS MK04X, slave.board IS MK04X:
VAL hostlink IS 2:
VAL no.processors IS 5:
[no.processors]CHAN OF ANY ring:
}}}
PLACED PAR
  PROCESSOR 1 T8
    {{{   placement for master
    PLACE ring[0] AT link3in :
    PLACE ring[1] AT link1out:
    }}}
    master(master.board, hostlink, ring[0], ring[1])
  PLACED PAR i=2 FOR (no.processors-1)
    PROCESSOR i T8
      {{{   placement for slave
      PLACE ring[i-1]             AT link3in :
      PLACE ring[i\no.processors] AT link1out:
      }}}
      slave(slave.board, ring[i-1], ring[i\no.processors])
}}}
...F code
...F descriptor
...F CODE PROGRAM multi_transputer.tsr
}}}
```

The ring of transputers is taken to comprise a master transputer (connected
directly to the host transputer) and four slave transputers. The structure
of the PROGRAM is generic.

1. The configuration (top) level consists of the definitions of the separately compilable processes master and slave, definitions of param-

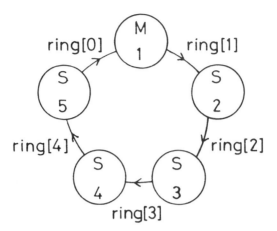

Figure 2.2: One-directional ring consisting of a master and four slaves

eter values, channel declarations and, finally, the placement information following the PLACED PAR statement.

2. Processes which are to run on different transputers *must run in parallel*. PLACED PAR specifies this, being logically the same as PAR, but
   contains additional placement information, namely:

   - the PROCESSOR statement which specifies the processor type and
     identifier on which a particular instance of one of the SCs is to
     be run; the identifier value is an arbitrary integer, but note that
     the process master (with direct connection to the host) must be
     the first in *textual order*.

   - the hard channel placement using the keywords PLACE...AT...
     which allocate an occam channel to the physical address of a
     transputer link; for clarity the link addresses are given meaning-
     ful names which are defined in the fold

```
{{{ link definitions
VAL link0out IS 0:
VAL link1out IS 1:
VAL link2out IS 2:
VAL link3out IS 3:
VAL link0in  IS 4:
VAL link1in  IS 5:
VAL link2in  IS 6:
VAL link3in  IS 7:
}}}
```

- the particular instance of the process, with actual parameters that have either been assigned values in the list of definitions (e.g. `hostlink`) or are channel names that have been placed at hard links in the immediately preceding set of `PLACE...AT...` statements.

3. `PLACED PAR` may be *replicated* in the obvious way and the replicator index used to assign values to the replicated processor identifiers. This is the way that multiple copies of one process can be distributed over an array of transputers. The replicator index is also used to identify channel connections.

4. Note that in the full placement each occam channel must appear exactly twice, once assigned to an input link and once assigned to an output link.

5. At the configuration level, all constants must be of type `VAL` and all channels of type `CHAN OF ANY`.

6. Note the use of the constant `no.processors` which allows the `PROGRAM` to be reconfigured for any number of processors (greater than one) by changing only one line.

2.5.2 Master Template

The fold ... `SC master.tsr` is opened below.

```
{{{  SC master.tsr
{{{F master.tsr
PROC master(VAL INT board, hostlink, CHAN OF ANY in, out)
  ...  system libraries
  ...  PROC bucket.master
  CHAN OF ANY keyboard, screen, debug, mouse:
  [4]CHAN OF ANY from.filer, to.filer:
  PAR
    masterSys(keyboard, screen, debug, mouse,
              from.filer, to.filer, board, hostlink)
    bucket.master(keyboard, screen, debug, in, out)
  :
}}}
...F master.dcd code
...F master.dds descriptor
...F master.dlk link
...F master.ddb debug
}}}
```

It is similar to the previous examples in the way in which it bundles a
user process (in this case bucket.master) with a system process running
in parallel. The major difference is that the formal parameter list now
contains two additional channels (in and out) which connect master to
neighbouring processes around the ring.

The following user process (defined in the fold PROC bucket.master) is
part of the simplest distributed program imaginable: a 'bucket brigade'.

```
PROC bucket.master(CHAN OF ANY keyboard, screen,
                                debug, in, out)
  INT char:
  SEQ
    keyboard ? char
    out ! char
    in ? char
    screen ! char
    Writes(screen, "*C*N")
  :
```

It is the controlling process which takes a character value from the keyboard, sends it around the ring of processors, receives it back again and outputs it to the terminal screen.

2.5.3 Slave Template

Since the only I/O facility on a slave transputer is to output messages to the supervisor bus (it does not have a direct connection to the host) its system process, slaveSys, is simpler than the master system process. The template, shown below, is correspondingly simpler, although the structure should be familiar by now.

```
{{{  SC slave.tsr
{{{F slave.tsr
PROC slave(VAL INT board, CHAN OF ANY in, out)
   ...   system libraries
   ...   PROC bucket.slave
  CHAN OF ANY debug:
  PAR
    slaveSys(debug, board)
    bucket.slave(debug, in, out)
:
}}}
...F slave.dcd code
...F slave.dds descriptor
...F slave.dlk link
...F slave.ddb debug
}}}
```

debug is the channel for outputting messages to the supervisor bus. Again the formal parameter list contains the channels in and out which connect slave to the ring. bucket.slave, defined in the fold ... PROC bucket.slave, is the simple process

```
PROC bucket.slave(CHAN OF ANY debug, in, out)
  INT char:
  SEQ
    in ? char
    out ! char
:
```

which passes a single character value from the channel in to the channel out.

A more sophisticated distributed PROGRAM with more involved ring communications, which builds on this example, is described in chapter 3. Before that, a useful exercise would be to modify the bucket brigade program so that each slave sends Hello from slave number followed by its own identifier around the ring and onto the terminal screen.

Chapter 3

Case Study: Cellular Automata

3.1 Introduction

The purpose of this chapter is to discuss how to implement an occam program on a network of transputers. The example chosen is that of a *1-dimensional cellular automaton*. This is conceptually very simple, has a high degree of parallelism and produces interesting pictures on a simple VDU screen.

Cellular automata are discussed in some generality in chapter 4, where it is emphasized that they constitute a generic class of problems for parallel computers. Here, we focus on the simplest of them, as this exposes the structure of the program, and especially the communications harness, without the distraction of complicated calculations. You will see that parallel implementations of this type crop up quite often in real applications.

The cellular automaton we are going to simulate consists of a linear chain of cells with periodic boundary conditions (i.e. a closed ring). Each cell may exist in one of two states, 0 or 1, represented by ' ' and '*', respectively, on the terminal screen. The system starts off with any initial state input from the keyboard by the user. It subsequently evolves in discrete time steps in which every cell is updated simultaneously according to a simple rule, and the new state is drawn on the next line of the screen. The rule is that the state of each cell is given by the sum of the states of itself and its two nearest neighbours at the previous time step, modulo 2.

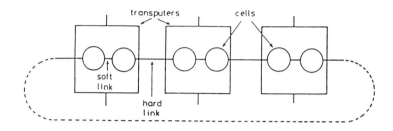

Figure 3.1: Geometric decomposition of 1-dimensional cellular automaton

3.2   The Process for One Cell

The obvious way to map this problem onto a network of transputers is *geometrically* (see chapter 4) i.e. put consecutive groups of cells on consecutive transputers connected in a closed ring, as shown in figure 3.1. This uses up two of the links on each transputer. At least one transputer (the *master*) will have to take charge of I/O from the keyboard and to the terminal screen, but either of the two spare links are available for this. On a Computing Surface, for example, the master would be connected directly to the *host*, but this will be considered further when we discuss placement.

Let us begin by considering the process which will reside on any one of the *slaves*. This will consist of processes for some number of cells, *running in parallel* (this is just the physical situation). All the cell processes are identical. Each cell process must first input its initial state, and then perform a sequence of updates (taking information about the states of neighbouring cells from neighbouring cell processes). After every update, each cell must send its current state to the master for outputting to the terminal screen. Finally, the cell must be ready at all times to receive a message, originating from the master, telling it to terminate. Adopting a 'top-down' approach to this program, the cell process might look like this:

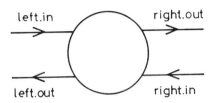

Figure 3.2: Soft channels for a cell

```
PROC cell (CHAN OF ANY left.in, left.out,
                       right.out, right.in)
  {{{ PROCs
  ... initialise
  ... update
  ... send.state
  }}}
  INT state :
  BOOL running :
  SEQ
    initialise(left.in, right.out, state)
    running := TRUE
    WHILE running
      SEQ
        update(state)
        send.state(left.in, right.out, state, running)
  :
```

Here the channels in and out of the cell are labelled as shown in figure 3.2. The simplest process to describe is **update**, which broadcasts the current state of the cell (called **state** in the above program) to its neighbours *in parallel* with inputting the states of its neighbours. It is essential that these processes run in parallel to avoid *deadlock*. Once these communications have taken place, the cell may update its state using the rule described in section 3.1. The occam process for this is:

```
PROC update (INT state)
  INT left.state, right.state :
  SEQ
    PAR
      left.in ? left.state
      left.out ! state
      right.in ? right.state
      right.out ! state
    state := (state + (left.state + right.state)) REM 2
  :
```

Next, it is necessary to make some decision about how the operation of the cell process is to be controlled from outside (by the master). The way this example is set out, there is a *single bi-directional chain* for communicating both data (cell states) and commands from the master. So it is necessary to invent some sort of *protocol* to distinguish these two types of data. The obvious thing to do is recognise that cell states are either 1 or 0 and therefore to use any other integer values for commands.

As an example, consider the process initialise which inputs the initial state of the cell. We presume that the master inputs the initial state of the cellular automaton from the keyboard, converts it into a stream of 1s and 0s, and outputs it around the ring. The first cell process takes the first integer it receives as its initial state and passes the rest on around the ring. If it receives an integer which is bigger than 1, it interprets it as an 'end of initial state', passes this on around the ring, in order to terminate the other cells, and then terminates itself. The other cells do the same thing. The process is given below.

```
PROC initialise (CHAN OF ANY in, out, INT state)
  SEQ
    in ? state
     IF
      state > 1
        SEQ
          out ! state
          state := 0
      TRUE
        BOOL inputting :
        INT x :
        SEQ
          inputting := TRUE
          WHILE inputting
            SEQ
              in ? x
              IF
                x > 1
                  SEQ
                    out ! x
                    inputting := FALSE
                TRUE
                  out ! x
  :
```

This code allows for the possibility of an incomplete initial state being sent out by the master: cells which receive an 'end of initial state' command instead of a 1 or 0, set their initial state to 0.

Following the command structure outlined above, the cell process may be completed with

```
PROC send.state (CHAN OF ANY in, out,
                 VAL INT state, BOOL running)
  INT x :
  BOOL talking :
  SEQ
    talking := TRUE
    WHILE talking
      SEQ
        in ? x
        IF
          x > 1
            SEQ
              out ! state; x
              talking := FALSE
          x < 0
            SEQ
              out ! state; x
              talking := FALSE
              running := FALSE
          TRUE
            out ! x
  :
```

This implements the final piece of the command structure, which will terminate the cell process on receipt of a negative integer, having previously
output its final state followed by the negative integer in order to terminate
the other cells further around the ring. The first process to terminate is
the first in the ring, the last process to terminate is the master, after it
has received the final state of the automaton and output it to the terminal
screen.

3.3   Connecting Processes Together and I/O

The reader is encouraged to do this as an exercise. In the next section
the placement for a PROGRAM on a ring of transputers is discussed. This is
appropriate if you have access to more than one transputer. The exercise
is equally viable as an EXE on a single-transputer workstation. In fact the
PROGRAM might be developed first as an EXE and only later PLACED on a
ring.

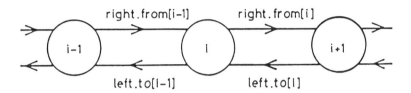

Figure 3.3: Channel names in placement for a bi-directional ring

The cell process is complete (unless you choose to change the control structure). You will need to write a master process which handles I/O with your terminal and sends appropriate commands around the ring. One solution which we call cell.master is given in section 3.5. You might decide, initially, to restrict the freedom of the user to choose arbitrary initial conditions (e.g. setting up the initial state in the master, rather than inputting it from the keyboard) and to terminate the program at will (e.g. fixing the number of time steps). In some sense, the most elementary initial states are either a random sequence of 0s and 1s, or a single nonzero cell.

Also, depending on how many transputers you include in your ring, you may choose to have one, two, or more cell processes per transputer, in order that your cellular automaton picture approximately fills your terminal screen. Note that if you place more than one cell on each transputer, some of the channels left.in, left.out, right.in and right.out will be *soft channels* internal to one transputer, while others will be PLACED AT hard links. In the extreme case of an EXE all the processes, cell.master and cell, reside on the same processor and communicate via soft channels. This in no way alters the logical structure of the program.

3.4   Ring Placement

In discussing a placement we will continue to assume, as in chapter 2, that the PROGRAM is *booted from within* OPS. Hence there is no placement required for the host transputer which runs only system code. An appropriate arrangement of soft channels and processes is shown schematically in figure 3.3. The corresponding placement is

```
...  SC master.tsr
...  SC slave.tsr
{{{  declarations
...  Meiko board types
...  link definitions
{{{  parameter values
VAL hostlink IS 2:
VAL master.board IS MK04X, slave.board IS MK04X:
VAL no.processors IS 81:
}}}
{{{ channel declarations
[no.processors]CHAN OF ANY right.from, left.to :
}}}
}}}
PLACED PAR
  PROCESSOR 1 T8
    PLACE right.from[0] AT link3in  :
    PLACE left.to[0]    AT link3out :
    PLACE right.from[1] AT link1out :
    PLACE left.to[1]    AT link1in  :
    master(master.board, hostlink, right.from[0],
           left.to[0], right.from[1], left.to[1])
  PLACED PAR i = 2 FOR (no.processors-1)
    PROCESSOR i T8
      PLACE right.from[i-1]              AT link3in  :
      PLACE left.to[i-1]                 AT link3out :
      PLACE right.from[i\no.processors]  AT link1out :
      PLACE left.to[i\no.processors]     AT link1in  :
      slave(slave.board, right.from[i-1], left.to[i-1],
      right.from[i\no.processors], left.to[i\no.processors])
```

Note that to be useful a channel name should convey three pieces of information: the location of its two ends and the direction that data flows along it.

In the above example, SC slave.tsr is the slave template in which has been embedded a user process comprising one or more copies of cell; SC master.tsr is the master template incorporating the cell.master process (described in the next section). The templates are described in chapter 2.

3.5 Master Process for the Cellular Automaton

The cell.master process for the cellular automaton requires, in addition to the ring channels, access to the channels keyboard, screen and debug. In the code for cell.master given below, these are included as formal channel names in the procedure definition and provide the *plumbing* into the system code in the master template.

The toplevel of cell.master is

```
PROC cell.master(CHAN OF ANY keyboard, screen, debug,
                 left.in, left.out, right.out, right.in)
  ... PROC send.state
  INT flag:
  SEQ
    ...  input state
    ...  run until signalled to terminate
  :
```

The input state process inputs characters from keyboard until a character other than ' ' or '*' is encountered. The process initialise, running in each cell, handles the case when too few initial states are input. If too many are received, these are absorbed by the code in the fold called check for excess characters.

```
{{{  input state
PAR
  BOOL inputting:
  SEQ
    inputting := TRUE
    WHILE inputting
      INT char:
      SEQ
        keyboard ? char
        IF
          char = (INT ' ')
            right.out ! 0
          char = (INT '**')
            right.out ! 1
          TRUE
            SEQ
              right.out ! 2
              inputting := FALSE
  {{{  check for excess characters
  BOOL checking:
  SEQ
    checking := TRUE
    WHILE checking
      SEQ
        left.in ? flag
        IF
          flag = 2
            checking := FALSE
          TRUE
            SKIP
  }}}
}}}
```

The run until signalled to terminate fold is opened below.

```
{{{  run until signalled to terminate
BOOL running:
SEQ
  running := TRUE
  WHILE running
    INT any:
    PRI ALT
      keyboard ? any
        SEQ
          right.out ! -1
          running := FALSE
          send.state (left.in, screen)
      TRUE & SKIP
        INT right.state, left.state:
        SEQ
          right.in ? right.state
          left.out ! right.state
          left.in ? left.state
          right.out ! left.state
          right.out ! flag
          send.state (left.in, screen)
}}}
```

The interrupt from keyboard is placed at high priority to ensure that it gets noticed. A cell process has not been included in cell.master, although it might have been, so the master must act as a message-passer between the cells on its left and right.

Finally, the process send.state is used to output the latest state of the automaton to screen. Note that it is not the same as the process of the same name running on each cell.

```
{{{ PROC send.state
PROC send.state (CHAN OF ANY in, out)
  BOOL running:
  SEQ
    running := TRUE
    WHILE running
      INT x:
      SEQ
        in ? x
        IF
          x = 0
            out ! INT ' '
          x = 1
            out ! INT '**'
          TRUE
            SEQ
              out ! INT '*N'
              running := FALSE
  :
}}}
```

Chapter 4

Parallel Algorithms

4.1 Introduction

Parallel architectures of the MIMD (Multiple Instruction Multiple Data) type, and particularly distributed-memory systems like the transputer, offer a modular approach to the construction of computers which may be tailored to suit individual applications. [1] Further, parallel processing offers a speed-up beyond the technological limitations on single-processor systems which, at the high-performance end, may be an order of magnitude more cost-effective than vector supercomputers. Most manufacturers in this sector of the market now embrace parallel processsing to some degree.

Ideally, a program runs N times faster on N processors than on a single processor, although the actual speed-up may be much less. The design of algorithms to achieve this sort of speed-up is an active area of research. Since the algorithm, programming language and hardware are intimately connected, this exercise is difficult to carry out in generality. Occam and the transputer constitute an environment in which these questions can be addressed and, in a growing number of cases, answered. Unfortunately, parallel computers are not very forgiving; the difference between the performance of a good and a bad program is much greater than for a serial computer. The crux of the matter is not the writing of a program, but the way in which an application is mapped onto the architecture. To do this efficiently you must *'think parallel'*.

Not only do the normal considerations of numerical analysis apply, (and they must often be reappraised because a successful serial algorithm can be

---

[1] In this chapter SIMD (Single Instruction Multiple Data) machines like the DAP and Connection Machine, and shared-memory machines like the Butterfly will be largely ignored.

a disastrous parallel algorithm) it is also necessary to take account of

- how data is to be distributed in memory;
- how computations are distributed among processors;
- inter-processor communications;
- inter-processor connections, if reconfigurable.

The aim is to match the parallelism of the algorithm to the parallelism of the computer in such a way as to minimise the execution time of the program. At any stage within an algorithm, the *parallelism of the algorithm is the number of operations that are independent and can therefore be performed concurrently*. This may vary from stage to stage. The *natural hardware parallelism is the number of processors that may run concurrently*, including both arithmetic and link processors on the transputer. In devising parallel algorithms we are concerned with maximising

$$\text{efficiency} \quad = \quad \frac{t_1}{N \times t_N}$$

$$t_1 \quad = \quad \text{time taken by program on one processor}$$

$$t_N \quad = \quad \text{time taken by program on N processors}$$

by *balancing the loads* on the various processors, i.e. we want all the processors to be doing *useful* work most of the time. If the time taken routing data between the processors is comparable to the arithmetic operation time, then it will play an important role in the choice of algorithm. In fact, at the present time the key factor is the ratio of the computation and communication speeds. Communication technology is lagging behind computation technology and on parallel machines currently on the market many applications are *communications bound*. This may not always remain so; several manufacturers are developing routing chips to handle message passing without taking up processor cycles.

For some time yet users will not be able to rely on a smart compiler to map applications onto the hardware automatically. In many cases the parallelism in the application is obvious, as is the case for most linear algebra problems such as solving a system of linear equations, for the simulation of physical systems described by partial differential equations which lead to local update rules, and, say, for simulating a factory. Then the problem is to exploit the parallelism, rather than to introduce it.

In general, the mapping is not so obvious, although there are plenty of situations in the real world where parallel processing is the preferred method: a word-processing pool, an airline check-in, a production line, a building site, etc.

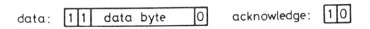

Figure 4.1: Communication packets

4.2 Transputer Hardware

Before describing some elementary strategies for parallel processing, it is helpful to have an overview of the 'target' architecture. The transputer is the *'computer on a chip'* (processor, memory and communications) built by Inmos Ltd; hence the name, which is a composite of *'transistor'* and *'computer'*. It is a *programmable building block for concurrent systems*, spanning a wide range of system sizes from microcomputer to supercomputer.

The transputer implements the *process model of computation* embodied in its native language occam. Although transputers may be programmed in other languages, occam is the most efficient. The transputer architecture is *wordlength independent* so that transputers of different wordlengths may be interconnected and programmed as a single system. Since all *memory is local*, the memory bandwidth grows in proportion to the number of transputers. Each transputer has an external memory interface which extends the address space into off-chip memory (it can be arranged for frequently-accessed data to be stored on chip).

Transputers use *point-to-point communication links*. Every member of the transputer family has one or more standard links which may be connected to links on other transputers to build networks of various sizes and topologies. Hence, the communications bandwidth does not saturate as more transputers are added. Each link provides *synchronous bi-directional communication* corresponding to two occam channels, one in each direction.

Communication via any link may occur concurrently with communication on all other links and with program execution. An occam program is the same regardless of whether it involves communication between processes executing on different transputers or on a single transputer. More generally, a program intended for a network of transputers, may be compiled and executed on a single transputer, which shares its time between the concurrent processes. A process which is waiting for communication or timeout does not consume any processor time.

A message is transmitted as a sequence of bytes, each sandwiched between two *'start bits'* and a *'stop bit'*, as in figure 4.1. After transmitting a data byte, the sending link controller waits until an *acknowledge* (see fig-

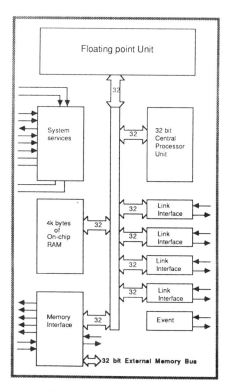

Figure 4.2: Schematic diagram of a transputer

ure 4.1) has been received. In the recent versions of the transputer, the
receiving link controller can transmit an *acknowledge* as soon as it starts
to receive a data byte, so transmission can be continuous (early versions
did not send the acknowledge until after the byte had been received). This
protocol synchronises communication of each byte, ensuring that slow and
fast transputers, and transputers of different wordlength, can communicate
reliably.

After reset, a transputer waits for the first message to be received on a
link, and interprets this as a program to be loaded and executed. This provides the standard mechanism for bootstrapping a network of transputers.
It is also possible to bootstrap from external ROM.

Figure 4.2 is a schematic diagram of a transputer. There are essentially
three types of transputer:

T212 a 16 bit, 10 MIPS processor with 2 KByte of memory;

T414 a 32 bit, 10 MIPS processor with 2 KByte of memory and sustainable 32 bit floating-point performance of around 80 Kflops;

T800 a 32 bit, 10 MIPS processor with 4 KByte of memory, a 64 bit floating-point co-processor capable of sustaining around 1 Mflops in 32 bit arithmetic.

All are single 1.5μ CMOS chips with a reduced instruction set architecture, supporting 4 Inmos standard, full duplex, serial links (10 or 20 Mbit/sec each), and operating at several speeds (typically 20 MHz). Inmos supplies *link adaptors* which interface transputers to non-transputer devices. A low frequency clock (5 MHz) is used irrespective of the performance of the transputers. Each transputer increments a timer which may be read in occam and used, for example in real-time systems, to determine the activity of a process. Communication depends on frequency not phase, so transputers with independent clocks can communicate reliably. There are compilers for C, FORTRAN and PASCAL.

The transputer allows a programmer complete control over the type of parallelism incorporated in a program (a responsibility for which the user may not be entirely grateful!) No program will have a unique mapping onto an MIMD array. This chapter will describe the basic strategies for parallel computation and point to some examples of successful implementations; these fall roughly into the following three classes:

Event Parallelism in which each processor executes a program *in isolation* from all the other processors.

Geometric or Data Parallelism in which each processor executes the same program on *data corresponding to a subregion of the system* being simulated and communicates boundary data to neighbouring processors handling neighbouring subregions.

Algorithmic Parallelism in which each processor is responsible for *part of the algorithm*, and all of the data passes through each processor.

4.3 Event Parallelism

4.3.1 The Task Farm

One of the simplest, and often the most efficient, ways of exploiting parallel processing is to distribute independent tasks to each of the processors. Such a configuration of the system may be called a *task farm*, and in general it will consist of a *master* processor, whose job it is to distribute the tasks and

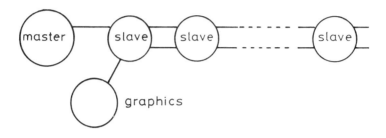

Figure 4.3: A transputer pipeline.

collect the results, and some number of *slave* processors, which actually do
the work. Many different organisations of processors are possible, e.g. a
tree with the master as a root, or a continuous chain beginning with the
master, as shown in figure 4.3. Of course, other processors may be added,
for example to handle external I/O, graphics, or to perform a statistical
analysis of the results from each of the tasks.

In the simplest situation, each slave processor executes the *same serial
program* on its own data set. The assignment of tasks by the master processor becomes part of the operating system and can be made transparent
to the user. All that the user needs to supply is a serial program and some
number of data sets requiring processing. In order to make efficient use
of a large processor array in this way, the number of data sets should be
very large. If the data sets themselves are large, the major difficulty is in
achieving sufficiently fast data-transfer rates between magnetic tapes, or
disks, and the slave processors, so that none of them is held up waiting for
others to read or write data. This may be solved using distributed mass
storage devices, each associated with a small group of slave processors and
controlled by some peripheral processor. In the situation in which the I/O
bandwidth is high enough, such a task farm can achieve a speed-up relative
to one processor equal to the number of processors.

A rather more sophisticated operating system would permit more than
one user program to run on a task farm at any one time, each user being
allocated a portion of the farm. The benefit perceived by the user would
then be increased *throughput*. It would be important, under such circum-

Figure 4.4: A ray-traced image produced on the ECS

stances to be able to trap wayward programs to prevent them corrupting others.

4.3.2 Ray Tracing

Another variant on the task-farm approach, is when a single computation can be divided up into many independent sub-tasks which can be farmed out amongst the slaves. A successful implementation of this is ray tracing, which is a way of displaying 3-dimensional pictures on a 2-dimensional screen (Dettmer 1986), an example of which is shown in figure 4.4. This involves setting up the 3-dimensional 'world', i.e. the objects which are to be viewed through the screen, and then devising a mapping of this onto the screen.

The basic idea behind ray tracing is to reproduce what happens in a pinhole camera. The image on the screen is built up from rays of light, coming from the objects, which pass through the pinhole. These rays may be identified by starting at a pixel on the screen and tracing back, through the pinhole, onto a surface in the 3-dimensional world. Each ray is then reflected backwards to determine whether it comes from another surface or from a light source. This backward tracing continues until the ray ends at a light source or passes out of the world. Once the source of a ray has been identified, the path of the ray is retraced from the source to determine

Figure 4.5: Photograph of the Mandelbrot set.

the colour and brightness of the corresponding pixel on the screen. The complete picture is built up by tracing one ray for each pixel. The paths of the reflected rays and the levels of illumination depend on the nature of the light source (e.g. *ambient light*, which is uniform in all directions, or *point sources*) and on the type of reflecting surface (e.g. *matt*, from which reflection is diffuse and in all directions, *smooth*, which reflects an incident ray as a cone of light, or *mirrored*, in which the light is reflected as a single ray); other optical effects, such as refraction by transparent objects, can also be included.

The ray tracing algorithm involves a great deal of computation. For each ray, the first task is to determine the point at which it strikes a surface in the 3-dimensional world. This involves solving a system of linear equations, given the equations of all the objects. The properties of the surface determine how the ray is reflected, and the procedure is repeated. This can become very complicated in the case of multiple reflections from smooth surfaces. Although computationally intensive, the algorithm is highly parallel as all of the rays are completely independent.

The arrangement of transputers in figure 4.3 is appropriate for this. Portions of the screen are distributed by the master transputer down the pipeline. The slaves all have a copy of the 'world'. Each slave takes a job from this stream, computes the image corresponding to that portion and sends the result back down the chain to the graphics processor.

4.3.3 The Mandelbrot Set

Much the same technique may be used to compute the mathematical structure known as the Mandelbrot set (Mandelbrot 1982). This has become established as something of a benchmark for MIMD computers, because the algorithm is easy to state and computationally intensive, involving many independent computations of varying length. Consequently, it is susceptible to the same parallel attack as ray tracing. The set has a very intricate, fractal structure, which can provide hours of artistic pleasure, provided portions of it can be computed quickly.

The set was discovered in 1980 by Mandelbrot, using computers at IBM. Figure 4.5 is a photograph of part of this set computed by the Edinburgh Concurrent Supercomputer. The picture represents part of the complex plane of the variable $c = p + iq$ (through coordinates p and q: $-2.25 < p < 0.75, -1.5 < q < 1.5$). For each pixel, which defines the value of c, the sequence of complex numbers z_n is generated via the feedback loop:

$$z_{n+1} = z_n^2 + c$$

Either the z's are attracted into a closed cycle, or they tend to infinity. The points that cycle correspond to values of c in the Mandelbrot set. So for each value of n, $r = |z_n^2|$ is computed. If $r > 100$ then choose colour n for that pixel and move on to the next pixel; if n is equal to the number of colours, set the pixel to black and go on to the next pixel; otherwise calculate a new z (see Peitgen 1986 for a fuller description of the algorithm).

Clearly, the number of times we go round the feedback loop varies from pixel to pixel. Each slave transputer in figure 4.3 may accept portions of the screen for computation, as distributed by the master. Provided the screen is divided up into many more small tasks than there are transputers in the chain, the algorithm naturally load-balances. Transputers given black areas take longer to complete than others, but no-one is held up waiting for their result. On the Edinburgh Concurrent Supercomputer, with 100 slave transputers, a 576×768 screen image is typically completed in a couple of seconds. Because of the high degree of parallelism, a linear speed-up with the number of processors is achievable over a wide range of system sizes.

4.4 Geometric Parallelism

4.4.1 Introduction

Geometry is based on the concept of distance, and the *geometric decomposition* of a problem divides the data up into subsets such that the data points in any one subset are in some sense closer to each other than to the data points in any other subset. The problem possesses *geometric parallelism* if, in addition, the algorithm involves only *local operations* i.e. connecting data points that are close together.

As an example, consider the computer simulation of a fluid. The region of space occupied by the fluid may be divided up into subregions, equal in number to the number of available processors. Each processor is given the responsibility of handling the fluid in one subregion. Because the behaviour of a tiny fluid element is determined only by the fluid elements immediately surrounding it (which exert forces on it), the evolution of the fluid in the interior of each region is determined entirely by data which is present in that processor's local memory. However, fluid may flow across the boundary of one subregion into the neighbouring subregion. The data corresponding to those fluid elements that flow across the boundary must be transferred between the memories of the processors handling the two subregions.

Typically then, there must be a transfer of surface data, while interior (or bulk) data remains local to a single processor. The amount of data which must be *transferred* relative to the amount which can be *processed internally* goes like the *ratio of the surface area to the volume*. This is directly related to the *balance of computation vs communication*. It is therefore important to pick subregions which have as small a surface area as possible for fixed volume. This maximises the likelihood that it will be possible to completely overlap communication of boundary data by computation using only bulk data.

The communication time is also proportional to the distance between processors. So, in order to keep down the communication time, the processors handling neighbouring subregions of the fluid should themselves be close together; ideally they should be neighbours. This completes the geometric decomposition i.e. *the processor array should have, as far as possible, the same geometry as the system being simulated.*

At this point two general questions may be raised:

1. The need for the processor array to have the same geometrical configuration as the system being simulated comes about because, at the present level of technology, *communication is expensive*. However, communication chips are being developed which can through-route messages intended for other processors with negligible delay and without interrupting their associated processor. The geometric decomposition onto arrays incorporating this technology will be much less restrictive. The aim is for such arrays to appear to the user as something like shared-memory machines, in which every processor can access every other processor's memory at negligible cost. If you can afford to wait a few years, then the problems of geometric decompo-

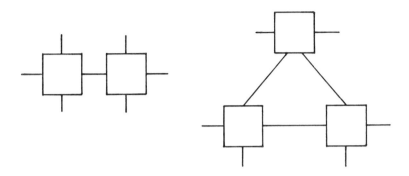

Figure 4.6: Examples of 6-link supernodes

sition need not concern you greatly! However, this solution is bound
to be expensive.

2. Transputers only have four links, and hence at most four nearest
   neighbours, yet the number of neighbours of a subregion in 3-dimensio-
   nal space (discretised on a regular cubic lattice) is six. It is clear
   that we cannot simply map subregions onto individual transputers,
   as implied above. One solution is to build *supernodes*, such as in figure 4.6. These have six links and could be used as building blocks for
   the processor array, with subregions being mapped onto supernodes.
   However, this introduces the extra complication of distributing the
   data in one subregion over the transputers within one supernode, a
   decomposition that may be far from 'natural', and of handling internal communications. The only alternative, until a transputer with at
   least 6 links appears on the market, is to use a 2-dimensional decomposition, in which 'vertical columns' are mapped onto a rectangular
   processor array.

Thus, in geometric parallelism a physical system is simulated on a *homogeneous* array of processors (or, supernodes). The same program runs
on each processor, operating on local data and transferring boundary data
to neighbouring processors as necessary. Of course, there will be a few
other processors running special tasks such as external I/O, monitoring
and data analysis. Each of the processors is brought into synchronisation
with its neighbour when boundary data is transferred. Since each processor

is doing approximately the same amount of work, this effectively brings the processors into something akin to lockstep, i.e. *SIMD mode*. It can be a highly efficient mode of operation for big problems, and is relatively simple to program because of the homogeneity. There may be difficulties if the algorithm requires global information at any stage, but this will be dealt with later.

4.4.2   Cellular Automata

Many problems in the computer simulation of systems in science and engineering can be tackled using geometric decomposition e.g. weather, wind tunnels, oil reservoirs, finite element analyses of structures, semiconductors, molecules, image processing, the interactions of elementary particles etc. The simplest of all, and arguably the most fundamental, are *cellular automata* (CA) (see Wolfram 1986 for a collection of modern papers on the subject).

CAs were invented by von Neumann around 1950 during his search for a self-replicating machine, i.e. a machine capable of constructing exact copies of itself, given an appropriate supply of material. He formulated the problem in terms of *uniform cellular space* i.e. space filled with cells, each of which may exist in a *finite number of states* including the empty state, and evolving by discrete time steps in lockstep, via *transition rules which depend only on the states of nearby cells*. Von Neumann was then able to prove that, if each cell could exist in one of 29 states and had 4 orthogonally adjacent neighbours, then there is a configuration of some 200K cells that contains a universal computer (Turing machine) and hence is a universal constructor.

Subsequently, many CA 'games' have been devised, in 1-, 2- and 3-dimensions, of which perhaps the most famous is Conway's 'Life' (Gardner 1970). There is apparently no limit to the application of CA ideas: from self-replicating moving automata resulting from complex transition rules in the primordial soup of amino acids, to board games like chess, image processing techniques, self-learning machines and even the universe itself. From our point of view, it is important to note that CAs model parallel computers, such as DAP and CLIP (Cellular Logic Image Processor). It is not surprising then that CA systems map very naturally onto parallel architectures and that the natural mapping is a geometric one.

The simplest CA consists of a line of cells $a_i, i = 1, \ldots, n$, with periodic boundary conditions ($a_{n+1} = a_1$), each of which can exist in one of two states $a_i = 0$ or 1. This system evolves in time according to a deterministic rule, applied simultaneously to every cell, whereby a_i at the next time step depends only on the present state of itself and its nearest neighbours i.e.,

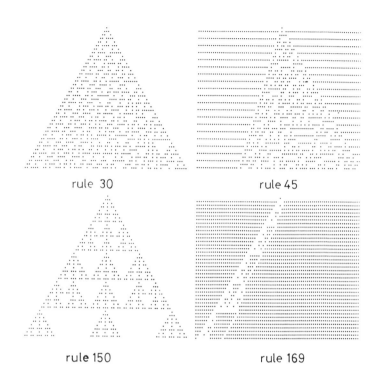

Figure 4.7: Examples of 1-dimensional CA patterns

in general,

$$a_i(t+1) = f(4a_{i-1}(t) + 2a_i(t) + a_{i+1}(t) + 1)$$

It is easy to see that there are 2^8 possible rules, labelled by rule numbers $r = 0$ to 255, such that $f(x)$ is defined to be the xth digit in the binary representation of r (reading from the least significant digit). Examples of the patterns generated from a single nonzero seed are shown in figure 4.7; clearly, there is a wide diversity of behaviour, even in such a simple system as this. [For drawing coloured pictures consider cells with a number of states equal to the number of colours and generalise the above rule accordingly (see Wolfram 1986).]

The simplest implementation of this algorithm is on a chain of transputers, as shown in figure 4.3 and described in chapter 3. An occam procedure which updates a cell may run in parallel with the updating of every other cell, communicating with left and right neighbours through channels. In the simplest mapping, one such procedure is placed on each transputer and the channels are mapped onto transputer links. Bigger CA systems may be simulated by placing more than one cell on each transputer, in which case some of the channels are internal soft channels (i.e. memory locations). Since there are two more spare links per transputer, these may be conveniently used to form a second chain containing the graphics processor, down which display information is sent. If the same links are used to pass both graphics and nearest-neighbour information, then these data packets must be preceeded by protocols to identify them and their destination. Clearly, it becomes easier to overlap communication by computation as the number of CAs per transputer increases.

If you spend any time exploring the different CA rules, you will quickly discover situations in which most of the cells are dead and any interesting activity is confined to a relatively small region. The geometric decomposition of the problem then results in most of the transputers doing no useful work.

This situation becomes even more pronounced in higher dimensions e.g. in Life. The rule for Life is the following. Each cell in a 2-dimensional square array may be alive or dead. Its transition to the next generation is determined by the states of the surrounding 8 cells: a live cell with 2 or 3 live neighbours survives into the next generation, otherwise it dies (of loneliness, or overcrowding); a dead cell surrounded by exactly 3 live neighbours gives birth and is alive in the next generation, otherwise it remains barren. Conway was seeking a model of bounded growth. However, there were some surprising configurations of live cells found, such as a 'glider gun' which emits a continuous stream of 'gliders' (groups of 5 live cells which travel with constant velocity), and a 'breeder' which endlessly produces 'glider guns'. An 'acorn' starting configuration has been found, which grows for 5206 cycles into a stable 'oak'. Thus a rich variety of behaviour is possible. It would be difficult to devise any decomposition other than the obvious geometric one which could efficiently compute all these different behaviours, particularly because any sophisticated algorithm is likely to make use of global information.

2-dimensional CA-like models cover some important applications, apart from these games. For example, much of image processing is to do with applying local cellular logic rules to picture elements. An application of potential importance for engineering has come from recent work on the Connection Machine which shows that CAs can be used to model the Navier-Stokes equations of fluid flow (see Wolfram 1986). In the simplest case, 2-dimensional flows are represented by CAs consisting of particles moving

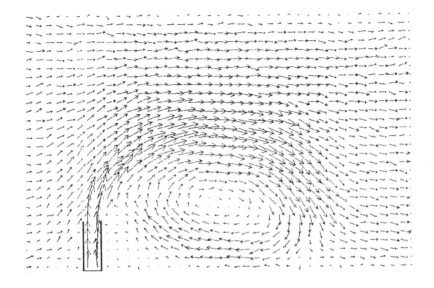

Figure 4.8: A cellular automaton fluid flow simulation

on a triangular lattice. The system evolves in discrete time-steps in which first each particle moves from one lattice site to the next in the direction of its velocity vector, then it collides with any other particles which arrive at the same site, conserving particle number and momentum. Hydrodynamic variables are computed by averaging over the particles in subregions of, say, 20 × 20 sites. Since the occupancy of any site is restricted to no more than one particle moving in each direction, the simulation can be efficiently coded in bits, or short integers, which together with the obvious geometric parallelism, makes it ideal for SIMD arrays like the DAP and Connection Machine. Figure 4.8 shows the result of simulating flow along a channel by this method on a Computing Surface. The channel is decomposed into strips transverse to the flow and each strip is processed by a different transputer, the transputers being connected to form a chain. Non-slip boundary conditions are implemented using special CA rules at the edges.

A similar type of simulation crops up in models of magnetism, except that probabilistic transition rules are necessary in order to represent thermal fluctuations. The simplest is the Ising model which restricts the atomic spin at each site of a regular lattice to the values 0 or 1. These spins interact with their nearest neighbours only, tending to align with them. The thermodynamics is generated by a Monte Carlo algorithm. The spin at each site flips between the two allowed values according to a probabilistic rule which depends on the energy change and the temperature.

In both the above examples, the configuration of the system is represented by a small number of bits at each site of a regular lattice and the variables evolve in parallel (though there is a subtlety in the thermodynamic case) in discrete time-steps according to local rules. The geometric decomposition consists of mapping subregions of the lattice onto a 2-dimensional array of transputers (neighbouring subregions onto neighbouring transputers) in the natural connectivity of a 'computing surface'. The actual shape of the transputer array may depend on the shape of the system being simulated e.g. an elongated rectangle, possibly a linear chain, for fluid flow down a channel, or a square array with periodic boundary conditions (obtained by joining links on opposite edges) for the Ising model. As regards the efficiency of these implementations, computation will completely overlap communication provided the subregions are large enough.

4.4.3   Partial Differential Equations

The situation when solving partial differential equations (PDE) by the method of *finite differences* is almost identical to that described above, except that floating-point arithmetic is used instead of bit-manipulation. The same sort of geometrical decomposition applies onto a processor array with the same geometrical configuration as the region of space (and time) in which the PDE is to be solved, and iterative solutions typically consist of the application of local transition rules.

As an example, consider the solution of Poisson's equation,

$$\nabla^2 u = f$$

for $u = u(x, y)$ in a rectangle, given the values of $f = f(x, y)$ everywhere and of u on the boundary. The first step is to replace space by a rectangular grid of points and the spatial derivatives by finite differences. The simplest approximation is to use the 5-point star stencil in figure 4.9. If the variables on the grid points are $u(i, j)$ etc., this means

$$\nabla^2 u \rightarrow u(i+1, j) + u(i-1, j) + u(i, j+1) + u(i, j-1) - 4u(i, j)$$

A relaxation algorithm for the solution rewrites the discretised Poisson equation as

$$u(i, j) = [u(i+1, j) + u(i-1, j) + u(i, j+1) + u(i, j-1) - f(i, j)]/4$$

in which it is assumed that the RHS is evaluated and used to overwrite the array element $u(i, j)$ corresponding to the *interior point* (i, j). If one of

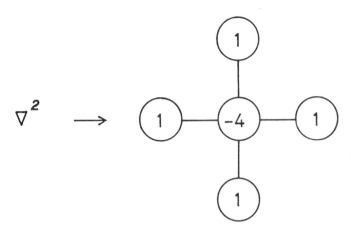

Figure 4.9: 5-point star stencil approximation to ∇^2

the points in this expression resides on the boundary of the region then its *constant* boundary value is used. This is a particularly simple example of a local update, or transition rule. Assuming this algorithm (Gauss-Seidel) converges fast enough to be practical, the parallel implementation is exactly the same as for the CAs.

Sometimes, because of poor convergence of relaxation methods, more sophisticated algorithms are required. These often make use of *global information*, such as the sum of the squares of variables like $u(i,j)$ at the grid points (e.g. the Conjugate Gradients algorithm for solving large sparse systems of linear equations, such as result from discretising the Poisson equation). Local sums may be computed by each processor, but then these values must circulate around the array in order to accumulate and distribute the global sum.

For an $L_1 \times L_2 \times L_3$ array connected as a 3-dimensional torus (i.e. periodic in each direction), an efficient way to do this is as follows. First, everyone sends their value in the 1-direction, adding values they receive to their partial sums and passing the values they receive on around the chain. After $L_1 - 1$ transfers, everyone in the same chain has the sum of all the local values in that chain. Next, the same thing happens in the 2-direction, with everyone circulating their local 1-direction partial sums, until everyone has the partial sum for the (1,2) plane in which they lie. This requires a further $L_2 - 1$ transfers. Finally, these partial sums are circulated in the 3-direction, to accumulate the global sum on every node. In total $L_1 + L_2 + L_3 - 3$ successive transfers are required (although each of these corresponds to $L_1 L_2 L_3$ transfers in parallel, which are completely overlapped because they are of identical size).

It is worth mentioning here that a distinction is sometimes made between *fine-grained* and *coarse-grained* parallelism. The former is appropriate for homogeneous arrays with, say, 1000 (relatively simple) processors such as the Computing Surface, the latter for a few 10s of (perhaps very sophisticated) nodes such as the hypercube machines with pipelined vector nodes. Geometric decomposition works for both, and in general the larger the subregion placed on a node, the greater the ratio of bulk computation to surface communication, and hence the higher the efficiency. However, the efficiency depends critically on the *balance between the computational power on each node and the communications bandwidth between nodes*. If a coarse-grained array and a fine-grained array are to simulate the same system, in the same real time, the coarse-grained array will have to transfer proportionately more data between nodes than the fine-grained system and so will require a higher bandwidth.

4.5   Algorithmic Parallelism

4.5.1   The General Situation

Here the algorithm is broken up into different parts which are assigned to different processors. Thus a *network of transputers* is constructed, each with its own special role to play, *through which all the data flows*, as in a factory production line. Typically, all the data is stored in the memory space of one transputer, which then naturally acts as controller for the rest of the array. It feeds data through the network of slave transputers, which need have only limited storage capacity and, in particular, may have no off-chip memory at all (hence lowering the cost of the system). Having constructed such a system, it may be replicated geometrically, as in the previous section, but now each node contains more than one transputer i.e. is a *supernode*.

There are a number of difficulties with algorithmic parallelism. One is that at different stages during the computation, different algorithms may apply, and a configuration of transputers optimised for implementing one algorithm is unlikely to be appropriate for another. For example, one algorithm may be used to generate a set of data and a different one used to analyse it. This problem is, of course, much reduced if the transputers are connected by a *dynamically reconfigurable switch*, the technology for which is becoming available. Otherwise, the data analysis must be done on a different group of transputers from those generating the data. Since analysis cannot typically proceed in parallel with data generation, either a duplicate of the data must be stored or data generation must be suspended during analysis. The latter is undesirable as it reduces efficiency.

Another difficulty to be solved is *how to get control data to each of the slave processors*, for example in order to initialise them at the start of the computation. Since each slave has a different job to do, it will expect to receive 'personalised' instructions. One way of accomplishing this is via a *package-routing* network which uses the same link configuration as during operation. A *packet* has a header indicating its destination and a data length. The data content of most of the packets originating from the master controller consists of an instruction code followed by some parameters. Similar packets may be used by the slaves to convey their status back to the master.

Finally, it may happen that one process dominates the execution time. If this process cannot be divided up amongst more than one processor, it alone will determine the throughput and constitute a *bottleneck*.

Obviously, this is the natural way to simulate a machine, a production process, or even a whole factory. The major obstacle to efficiency is load-balancing: the number of processors assigned to simulating each component must be carefully tuned.

4.5.2 Long-range Interactions

The applications considered up to now have involved only short-range interactions. This is typical of the finite difference method for solving partial differential equations, where updating the approximation to the field variable at each grid point requires only information about the field values at neighbouring grid points.

Problems with *long-range interactions* may also be implemented efficiently in parallel (Fox et al. 1984). As an example, consider the time evolution of the solar system. This is a 10-body gravitational problem in which the force between any two particles is given by Newton's law,

$$F_{ij} = G \frac{m_i m_j}{r_{ij}^2}$$

and we wish to evolve the 10 equations of motion for some period of time T. There are several new difficulties here. First, the large parameter is T and this cannot be divided up amongst a large number of processors. The best that can be done is to put one particle on each processor, unless the results from several different sets of initial conditions are required, in which case decomposition into particles and initial conditions permits efficient use of

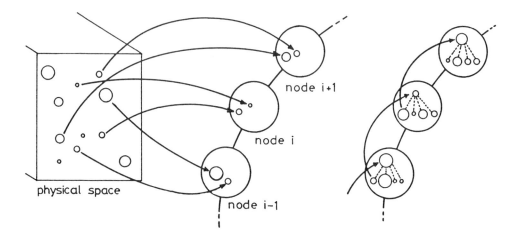

Figure 4.10: Algorithm for system with long-range forces

a larger processor array. The second difficulty is due to the fact that every particle interacts with every other.

In the direct method for evolving this system forwards in time, the total force on each particle, due to all the other particles, is computed, then each particle is moved forwards one time step and the process repeated. The computation is dominated by the calculation of the forces, because this is proportional to the square of the number of particles, whereas the timestepping grows only linearly with the number of particles. Since every particle interacts with every other, a geometric decomposition of the problem, in which the particles in different sub-regions of space are associated with different processors, is no use.

Instead, each processor is given the job of following the time evolution of one subset of the particles, which may be at widely scattered locations. In order to achieve load balancing, each processor is given the same number of particles to look after. This is illustrated in figure 4.10. The algorithm may be mapped onto any network of processors which incorporates a closed ring. The first step then is for each processor to pick one of its particles and send its mass and coordinates to the next processor around the ring. Next, each processor computes the force on its particles due to the incoming 'travelling' particle, and then sends the information about the travelling particle on to the next processor around the ring. This procedure is repeated until every particle has 'visited' every processor. This will be efficient provided the time taken to communicate a particle's data between processors is small compared to the time taken to compute the force it exerts on each of the particles in a processor. For a transputer system, it should be possible to completely overlap communication by computation. This obviously becomes easier to achieve as the number of particles per processor increases.

In particular, this situation pertains in the simulation of star clusters, where there may be tens of thousands of stars, and in the simulation of large collections of molecules if they interact through long-range forces, for example because they are electrically charged.

References

R. DETTMER *The artful transputer, Electronics & Power*, August 1986, 578.

G.C. FOX, and S.W. OTTO *Physics Today*, 37 No.5, 1984, 50.

M. GARDNER *Scientific American*, October 1970, 120.

H.-O. PEITGEN and P.H. RICHTER *The Beauty of Fractals*, (Springer-Verlag) 1986.

B.B. MANDELBROT *The Fractal Geometry of Nature*, (Freeman) 1982.

S. WOLFRAM *Theory and Applications of Cellular Automata*, (World Scientific) 1986.

Chapter 5

Further Examples

5.1   A Load-Balancing Pipeline

One form of parallelism which can be exploited well on a transputer-based machine is *event or task* parallelism, described in the previous chapter. Task parallelism is present where work can be divided into independent jobs, each of which can each be dealt with separately. By allocating each task to one of its n processors, a parallel computer can complete the tasks n times faster than a single-processor machine.

For example, it is often necessary to examine the behaviour of an object such as an airplane wing when it is driven at various frequencies. The obvious way to parallelise these calculations is to have different processors carry out calculations for different frequencies simultaneously. Each **worker** processor would store a complete copy of the airplane wing, while a single **master** processor would allocate frequencies to processors until all processors were busy (Figure 5.1). As soon as the worker finished calculations for its assigned frequency it would pass the results to the processor responsible for collecting them, and be given another frequency to work on.

The advantage of this approach is that if one worker takes a long time to do the calculations for a particular frequency, the other processors can carry on processing unhindered. The disadvantage is the large number of connections required by the master and results processors. What is needed is a scheme which requires only a small, fixed number of inter-processor links, but ensures that whenever a worker processor completes one task another is immediately available. A *load-balancing pipeline* is one way of doing this (see Figure 5.2).

In a load-balancing pipeline, each processor supports a *worker* process

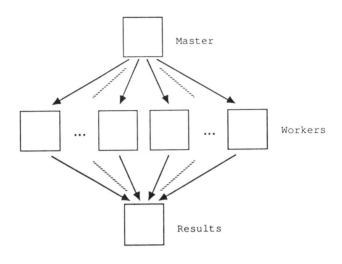

Figure 5.1: Master Allocating Tasks to Slaves

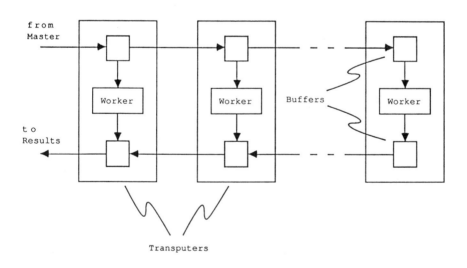

Figure 5.2: Overview of Pipe

which performs the calculations, and several *buffer* processes which carry tasks to workers and results to the display. Figures 5.3a-d shows how a load-balancing pipeline automatically distributes work. The remainder of this chapter describes how a load-balancing pipeline can be implemented using occam. It is important to note that only the communications and buffering need be implemented in occam; the portion of the code which is responsible for the calculations can be written in FORTRAN, C, or some other serial language, and then placed in an occam harness.

5.1.1   Preliminaries

Figure 5.4 shows the processes which reside on each processor in the load-balancing pipeline, and the communications channels which connect them. Each of these processes is described in detail below.

The most important feature of the arrangement of processes within each processor is that each hardware link has its own buffering process. Since inter-transputer communication is slower than communication between processes on the same transputer, it is important to ensure that no process is ever waiting on two hardware links, i.e. that hardware links never need to be synchronised with one another. Giving each hardware link its own buffering process is the simplest way to do this.

5.1.2   The Message-Passing Scheme

Before the processes shown in Figure 5.4 can be written, we must decide how messages are to be passed from one process to another. One requirement is *efficiency* — communication should consume as little time as possible. Another important requirement is *anonymity* — the message-passing procedures should not have to know anything about the contents of particular messages. This will allow most of the load-balancing pipeline code to be re-used in other programs.

For two reasons, these requirements prevent us from using a simple communications scheme such as:

Transmit	Receive
out ! a	in ? x
out ! b	in ? y
out ! c	in ? z

The first reason is that every time two transputers communicate there is a cost in setting up and synchronising the communication. Passing mes-

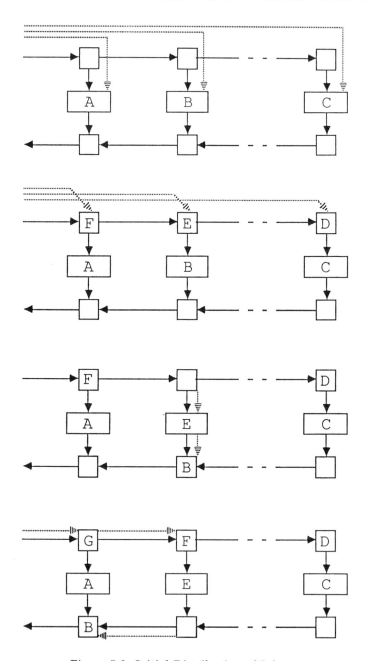

Figure 5.3: Initial Distribution of Jobs

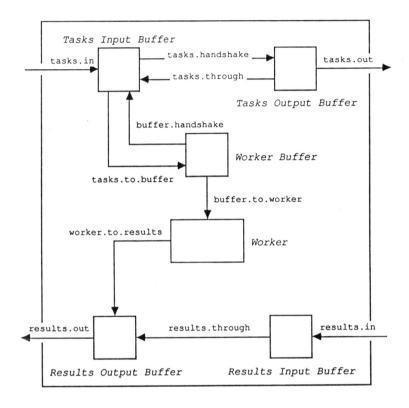

Figure 5.4: Processes Within Pipe Node

sages element by element would mean paying this set-up cost many times
for each message, so constructs such as this would not be efficient.

The second reason this scheme is bad is that the receiver must know
what type and size of message being sent. For example, the receiver above
must know that it is supposed to be reading exactly three integers. This
violates the anonymity requirement.

The first of these two problems is solved by packaging messages into
arrays and then sending whole arrays at once, using occam's array sub-
section notation:

```
Transmit                        Receive 2
--------                        ---------
chan ! [array FROM 0 FOR n]     chan ? [array FROM 0 FOR n]
```

Here,

```
[arrayname FROM start FOR count]
```

selects an array segment starting at index `start` and running for `count`
elements. This is more efficient than sending items one at a time because
the communications set-up cost is paid only once for each array portion
transmitted.

To prevent data type clashes, message arrays will always of type `INT`.
Users must *retype* array elements in order to send REAL32s, BYTEs, and
BOOLs, as in:

```
[256]INT msg :                  -- largest message ever sent
BOOL spare.bool RETYPES msg[0] :
REAL32 spare.r32 RETYPES msg[3] :
SEQ
  spare.r32 := 3.0 (REAL32)     -- actually goes in msg[0]
  msg[1] := 1                   -- goes in as written
  spare.bool := TRUE            -- actually goes in msg[2]
  chan ! [msg FROM 0 FOR 3]
```

The occam `RETYPES` statement allows variables to share locations in
memory, much as in a FORTRAN COMMON block.

Finally, to allow messages of varying sizes to be sent and received, the
message size will always be the first thing sent. Using this scheme, all
communication is of the form:

```
Transmit                        Receive
--------                        ---------
out ! n1                        in ? n2
out ! [array1 FROM 0 FOR n1]    in ? [array2 FROM 0 FOR n2]
```

occam allows communications protocols such as this to be implemented easily by providing *channel protocols*. For example:

```
PROTOCOL myProt IS INT;INT;INT :
CHAN OF myProt chan1, chan2 :
```

defines a protocol in which all messages are exactly 3 integers long, and then declares two channels which can only carry messages of that type. The protocol used by the load-balancing pipeline, in which each message contains a size followed by that many data items, is declared by:

```
PROTOCOL pipeProt IS INT :: []INT :
```

where the double colon :: means "an integer, followed by an integer array containing that many elements". Channels can then be declared to be of type pipeProt, and messages sent and received using:

```
Transmit                        Receive
--------                        ---------
out ! n1 :: array1              in ? n2 :: array2
```

5.1.3   The Processes

Worker – The Heart of the Pipeline

Worker is a simple process written in occam which accepts tasks, invokes whatever procedure the user has written to process these tasks, and then dispatches the results:

```
PROC Worker( CHAN OF pipeProt in, out )

  INT msg.size :
  [buffer.size]INT msg :

  WHILE TRUE
    SEQ
      in ? msg.size :: msg
      ProcessMsg( msg.size, msg )
      out ! msg.size :: msg
:
```

`ProcessMsg` is a user-written procedure which takes the data in the message, carries out some calculations, and writes its results back into `msg`, changing `msg.size` when it does so. `buffer.size` is a constant defined so that it will be in scope for all the procedure definitions given here. In most programs, `ProcessMsg` will be written in some language other than occam, for example C or FORTRAN. The compilers available for these languages on the Meiko Computing Surface contain functions providing access to channel communications, through which applications programs can interface with occam.

Results Input – A Simple Forwarding Buffer

The results input buffer is the simplest of the supporting buffers in the pipeline. It repeatedly reads messages from its input channel and forwards them to its output:

```
PROC FwdBuf( CHAN OF pipeProt in, out )

  INT msg.size :
  [buffer.size]INT msg :

  WHILE TRUE
    SEQ
      in ? msg.size :: msg
      out ! msg.size :: msg
:
```

It is important to realise that there is no busy waiting or polling going on here. When the input process

```
in ? msg.size :: msg
```

begins, `FwdBuf` is suspended until the link controller signals that there is a message to receive. Once the communication is initiated, the link's Direct Memory Access (DMA) engine handles the transfer of data autonomously, so that the transputer's CPU does not have to invest any effort in the buffering process. Similarly, `FwdBuf` is suspended while trying to output until there is something listening on the other end of its out channel. This scheduling and de-scheduling is handled automatically by the transputer's hardware.

Another feature of occam and the transputer highlighted by this simple process is that communication between two processes looks the same in occam regardless of whether the processes which are communicating are on the same transputer or are communicating through a hard link. Either, one, or both of in and out could be mapped onto an inter-transputer link without the program needing any recompilation.

Results Output – A Merging Buffer

The results output buffer is slightly more complicated than the simple forwarding buffer. This buffer must merge the stream of newly-calculated results from Worker, with those calculated by Workers on other processors. The ALT construct is used to do this:

```
PROC MergeBuf( CHAN OF pipeProt left, right, out )

  INT msg.size :
  [buffer.size]INT msg :

  WHILE TRUE
    SEQ
      ALT
        left ? msg.size :: msg
        right ? msg.size :: msg
      out ! msg.size :: msg
  :
```

Each pass around the loop, MergeBuf reads a message from either its left or right input channel, and then forwards the message on its output channel. As with FwdBuf, MergeBuf is automatically suspended when it cannot engage in communication.

Tasks Input – A Splitting Buffer with Handshaking

The tasks input buffer is the complement of the results output buffer. Rather than collating two streams, this buffer must split its input and send messages to whichever down-stream process is ready first.

It would seem obvious to use an ALT for this purpose as well, with the guard in the ALT being output processes:

```
ALT
  left ! msg.size :: size
  right ! msg.size :: size
```

However, output guards are not allowed inside an ALT. Their inclusion in the language would have made the design of the inter-transputer links much more complicated, and would have introduced too much non-determinism into the language.

To see why this is, consider the situation in Figure 5.5, equivalent to the following piece of pseudo-occam:

```
PAR
  ALT  -- process A
    c1 ! x
      SKIP
    c2 ! x
      SKIP

  ALT  -- process B
    c1 ? y
      SKIP
    c3 ? y
      SKIP

  ALT  -- process C
    c2 ? z
      SKIP
    c4 ? z
      SKIP
```

Process A becomes ready. It cannot simply transmit x to both processes B and C, because only one branch of an ALT is allowed to execute. A must therefore "warn" B and C that it is ready. If only one of B or C responds, then communication can go ahead. If both respond, A must decide where to send x, and must then tell the process not receiving x that it was all a mistake, A didn't really have anything for it, please carry on. Matters become even worse if we assume that after telling A that it was ready, C received something on channel c4 before A could transmit. C must then tell A to take x back, and to undo any calculations it has done since it sent x.

Input-only ALTs and handshaking are used to avoid this mess. Each process downstream from the SplitBuf must send a signal to the splitting buffer to indicate its readiness to receive a new message. Using this scheme, the splitting buffer is:

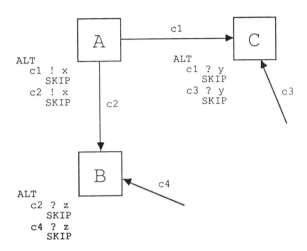

Figure 5.5: ALTing on Output

```
PROC SplitBuf( CHAN OF pipeProt in, left, right,
               CHAN OF INT      left.shake, right.shake )

  INT msg.size :
  [buffer.size]INT msg :
  INT handshake.signal :

  WHILE TRUE
    SEQ
      in ? msg.size :: msg
      ALT
        left.shake ? handshake.signal
          left ! msg.size :: msg

        right.shake ? handshake.signal
          right ! msg.size :: msg
  :
```

Since it is the presence of the handshake signal, not its value, which carries information, the handshake signal used is any single integer. This does not conform to the pipeProt protocol, so the right.shake and left.shake channels use a different protocol than the message-passing channels. This protocol is defined directly in the channel declaration by:

```
CHAN OF INT
```

SplitBuf can be improved slightly by considering what might happen during startup. By the time the first parcel of work arrives, handshake signals will be pending from both downstream processes. Since the choice between ALT branches is undetermined, a SplitBuf might very well forward the first work packet to reach it rather than sending it to its own worker process. If a large number of jobs are being processed, the effect of this will be negligible. In any case, it can easily be remedied by including two input statements (one for the message, and one for the handshake) and a single output statement before the WHILE loop to force the first message down a particular output channel:

```
SEQ
   in ? msg.size :: msg
   left.shake ? handshake.signal
   left ! msg.size :: msg
```

It is cumbersome to have to build into buffers such as MergeBuf and SplitBuf the number of input (or output) channels being serviced. General n-way multiplexing buffers can be built in occam by *replicating* the SEQ, PAR, and ALT constructs. A replicated SEQ, of the form:

```
SEQ i = 0 FOR n
   process
```

is equivalent to the FOR loop of many conventional languages, in that it carries out process n times sequentially. (The variable i is declared implicitly by its use as a replication index.) Similarly, a replicated PAR creates as many concurrent processes as specified, while a replicated ALT creates an n-way interrupt handler, as in:

```
PROC SplitBuf.n( CHAN OF pipeProt in,
                 []CHAN OF pipeProt out,
                 []CHAN OF INT handshake )

  INT msg.size :
  [buffer.size]INT msg :
  INT handshake.signal :
  VAL n IS (SIZE out) :

  WHILE TRUE
    SEQ
      in ? msg.size :: msg
      ALT i = 0 FOR n
        handshake[i] ? handshake.signal
          out[i] ! msg.size :: msg
:
```

Here, the output and handshake channels have been replaced by arrays
of channels of some unspecified dimension. SIZE is used to determine the
number of elements in these arrays.

Tasks Output and Worker Buffer – Forwarding with Handshaking

The tasks output buffer and worker buffer are both single-input, single-
output buffers which must handshake with the splitting buffer described
above. The code for these is the same:

```
PROC HandshakeBuf( CHAN OF pipeProt in, out,
                   CHAN OF INT      handshake )

  INT msg.size :
  [buffer.size]INT msg :

  WHILE TRUE
    SEQ
      handshake ! 0
      in ? msg.size :: msg
      out ! msg.size :: msg
:
```

The interactions between the two handshaking buffers and the splitting buffer are a good example of how cleanly occam handles inter-process
communication. Assume that the task output buffer has just forwarded a

message. It sends a handshake signal to the splitting buffer, which is suspended in its ALT (Figure 5.6a). The splitting buffer forwards its current message to the task output buffer and is then suspended again, waiting on input from the previous processor in the pipeline (Figure 5.6b).

Meanwhile, the Worker on this processor has taken the message stored in the worker buffer, which has therefore tried to send a handshake to the splitting buffer requesting more data (Figure 5.6c). This communication cannot take place, since the other process involved (the splitting buffer) is otherwise engaged. But as soon as the splitting buffer receives a message on its input channel and enters the ALT which picks up handshake signals, it notices the request from the worker buffer and forwards the new message to it (Figure 5.6d). This cycle of request/receive/forward continues *ad infinitum*.

5.1.4   Finishing Off

The Main Pipe Nodes

Having implemented the processes which make up a pipe node, we must now plumb these together. Two cases must be catered for: a node in the interior of the pipe, and a node at the end of the pipe. (Some sort of "master" node is also needed at the head of the pipe to send tasks to the pipe and dispose of the results, but as this is application-specific it is not described here.)

Though it may seem paradoxical, it is crucial in a load-balancing pipeline for the buffer processes in each pipe node to run at a higher priority than the worker process. The whole point of the load-balancing pipeline is that tasks can move quickly to available workers; each processor must therefore believe that passing jobs on to other processors further down the pipeline is more important than doing its own current task.

The cost of communications with high-priority buffers is actually quite low. As noted previously, once communication is initiated each link's DMA engine operates autonomously, allowing the CPU to carry on with other tasks. This means that only a few instructions have to be executed in each buffer process at a time.

occam includes a special form of the PAR statement to allow processes to be run with different priorities. In a PRI PAR, processes are assigned priorities according to their textual order[1]. Processes of a lower priority are scheduled only if no processes of a higher priority are ready to run. Using this, the normal pipe node sketched in Figure 5.4 is:

---

[1] A corresponding PRI ALT exists to provide prioritised interrupt handling.

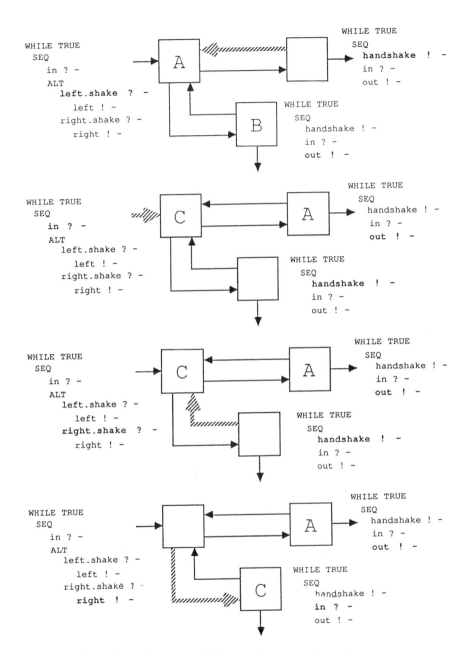

Figure 5.6: Sequence of Communications Operations

```
PROC MainNode( CHAN OF pipeProt tasks.in, tasks.out,
                                results.in, results.out )

  CHAN OF pipeProt tasks.through, results.through :
  CHAN OF pipeProt tasks.to.buffer, buffer.to.worker :
  CHAN OF pipeProt worker.to.results :
  CHAN OF INT      tasks.handshake, buffer.handshake :

  PRI PAR
    PAR
      SplitBuf( tasks.in,                 -- tasks in
                tasks.through, tasks.to.buffer,
                tasks.handshake, buffer.handshake )

      HandshakeBuf( tasks.through,    -- tasks out
                    tasks.out, tasks.handshake )

      HandshakeBuf( tasks.to.buffer, -- worker buffer
                    buffer.to.worker, buffer.handshake )

      FwdBuf( results.in,                 -- results in
              results.through )

      MergeBuf( worker.to.results,        -- results out
                results.through, results.out )

    Worker( buffer.to.worker, worker.to.results )
  :
```

One of the great strengths of occam is the ease with which it allows programmers to plumb together simple processes to create more and more complex processes. Now that MainNode has been written, it can be treated as a black box with two input and two output channels. It could be placed in parallel with other processes on a single processor, or used as a sub-process by a larger program which only spent part of its time as a load-balancing pipeline. By not distinguishing between inter- and intra-processor communications, occam provides a simple and powerful way to describe a wide range of concurrency.

The End of the Pipe

The end node of the pipe is shown in Figure 5.7. The worker and worker buffer processes are the same; since no splitting or merging needs to be done, simple forwarding buffers can be used for the task input and result output buffers:

```
PROC EndNode( CHAN OF pipeProt tasks.in, results.out )

    CHAN OF pipeProt tasks.to.buffer, buffer.to.worker,
                     worker.to.results :

    PRI PAR
      PAR
        FwdBuf( tasks.in, tasks.to.buffer )
        FwdBuf( tasks.to.buffer, buffer.to.worker )
        FwdBuf( worker.to.results, results.out )

      Worker( buffer.to.worker, worker.to.results )
    :
```

Placing Code on Processors

The last part of the program is a description which places processes on processors. Another specialised PAR, the PLACED PAR, is used to do this. Each branch of a PLACED PAR must contain a description of the processor, one or more *placement statements* describing how logical channels are to be mapped onto physical transputer links [2], and the name of the process that the transputer is to run.

Assuming that several transputers are connected as shown in Figure 5.8a, a placement statement for a pipeline containing num.slaves workers and a single master is:

---

[2] There must be at least one channel connection to each processor so that code may be booted down to that processor. For the same reason, it must be possible to trace a path from the root processor in a network (the one directly connected to the filestore) to each other processor in the network.

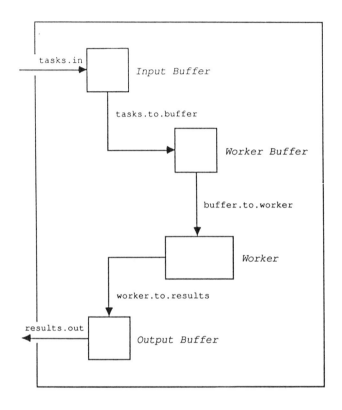

Figure 5.7: End Node of Pipeline

```
VAL link1Out IS 1 :        -- magic addresses
VAL link1In  IS 5 :        --   in transputer's
VAL link3Out IS 3 :        --   memory
VAL link3In  IS 7 :


[num.slaves]CHAN tasks, results :

PLACED PAR

  -- master
  PROCESSOR 0 T8
    PLACE tasks[0]   AT link1Out :
    PLACE results[0] AT link1In :
    master( tasks[0], results[0] )

  -- main pipe nodes
  PLACED PAR i = 1 FOR (num.slaves - 1)
    PROCESSOR i T8
      PLACE tasks[i-1]   AT link3In :
      PLACE results[i-1] AT link3Out :
      PLACE tasks[i]     AT link1Out :
      PLACE results[i]   AT link1In :
      MainNode(tasks[i-1], tasks[i], results[i],
              results[i-1])
  -- end pipe nodes
  PROCESSOR num.slaves
    PLACE tasks[num.slaves - 1]   AT link3In :
    PLACE results[num.slaves - 1] AT link3Out :
    EndNode(tasks[num.slaves - 1],
            results[num.slaves - 1])
```

As with buffer.size, num.slaves must be a constant defined somewhere so that it is in scope within the placement statement. The way this
placement maps onto the network of Figure 5.8a is shown in Figure 5.8b.
As new processors are made available, only the value of num.slaves in
the placement statement need be changed to allow the program to take
advantage of the extra hardware.

5.1.5 Stopping the Processes

One of the most difficult things to do cleanly in a multi-process environment
is stop processing. As written, the load-balancing pipeline's processes would

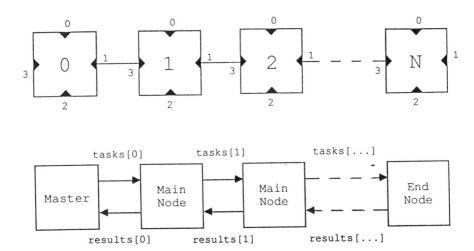

Figure 5.8: Placement of Processes on Processors

run forever. This section describes the modifications which must be made to each of the buffers previously described in order to allow them to terminate cleanly.

In the code descriptions below, the notation

        ... comment

will be used to indicate a section of code which has been "folded up". Folds such as this are a part of Meiko's Occam Programming System (OPS) and are used to structure code. In this section, they will be used simply to keep uninteresting code out of sight.

Identifying Messages

The first thing which must be added to the existing system is a way to distinguish termination messages from other messages. This is done by reserving part of the first word in each message for system use. In all messages, the top 16 bits of msg[0] will be used to store a set of flags classifying messages into types; the lower 16 bits of this word can then be used by particular applications. If a message is a termination command, a particular bit with symbolic name pipeStopFlag will be set. The test to see whether this flag is set will be modularised by putting it in a procedure testStopFlag, which sets a Boolean to TRUE or FALSE:

```
PROC testStopFlag( VAL []INT msg, BOOL stop )

  IF
    (msg[0] /\ pipeStopFlag) <> 0
      stop := TRUE
    TRUE
      stop := FALSE


:
```

Here, the use of VAL in a procedure parameter definitions shows that the parameter is read-only, while the /\ operator is occam's bit-wise logical AND.

The Forwarding Buffer

The forwarding buffer is the simplest of the processes described in the previous section. In its new incarnation it must check each message which it forwards to see whether that message was a termination command. FwdBuf must forward these termination messages to its output as usual so that termination can propagate down the pipeline.

```
PROC FwdBuf( CHAN OF pipeProt in, out )

  INT msg.size :
  [buffer.size]INT msg :
  BOOL loop, stop :

  SEQ
    loop := TRUE
    WHILE loop
      SEQ
        in ? msg.size :: msg
        out ! msg.size :: msg
        -- now test for termination
        testStopFlag( msg, stop )
        IF
          stop
            loop := FALSE
          TRUE
            SKIP
:
```

The Worker and the Handshaking Buffers

As far as termination is concerned, the worker process and the handshaking buffers are one-way pipes, each of which receive termination signals in one end and pass them along to the other. The terminating version of the handshaking buffer is created by modifying its non-terminating version exactly as FwdBuf was modified.

The terminating worker process is almost this simple as well. The only complication is that termination messages must be forwarded without being processed by ProcessMsg. This is handled by putting the ProcessMsg call in the appropriate branch of the IF which recognises termination messages:

```
testStopFlag( msg, stop )
IF
  stop
    loop := FALSE
  TRUE
    ProcessMsg(msg.size, msg)
```

The Splitting Buffer

The terminating version of the splitting buffer must behave somewhat differently than its non-terminating version. Task messages which enter a SplitBuf are passed to one or the other of the processes downstream from the SplitBuf. When a termination command arrives, on the other hand, it must be passed on to both downstream processes before the SplitBuf terminates.

```
PROC SplitBuf( CHAN OF pipeProt in, left, right,
               CHAN OF INT      left.shake, right.shake )

  ...  variable declarations

SEQ
  loop := TRUE
  WHILE loop
    SEQ
      in ? msg.size :: msg
      --  now test for termination
      testStopFlag( msg, stop )
      IF
        stop
          loop := FALSE
        TRUE
          ALT
            left.handshake ? handshake.signal
              left ! msg.size :: msg

            right.handshake ? handshake.signal
              right ! msg.size :: msg

  ...  forward termination message


:
```

Here, a message arrives and is tested to see whether it is a termination command. If it is, SplitBuf exits its forwarding loop and sends the message to both downstream processes concurrently. If it is not, it is passed on to one or the other downstream processes as before.

Sending the termination message downstream must be done carefully. Since the downstream processes do not know that the message is a termination command, destined for both of them, they will both be trying to send handshake signals to SplitBuf. If these signals are not accepted, the downstream processes will hang. SplitBuf will then hang in its turn, unable to forward the termination commands. Therefore, SplitBuf must accept the downstream processes' handshake signals before forwarding the termination command:

```
PAR
  SEQ  -- forward left
    left.handshake ? handshake.signal.left
    left ! msg.size :: msg
  SEQ  -- forward right
    right.handshake ? handshake.signal.right
    right ! msg.size :: msg
```

This code segments illustrates a very important feature of concurrent processes in occam. Two processes running concurrently must never try to write to the same variable at the same time; the effects of such a collision are unspecified, but almost invariably disastrous. For this reason, each branch of the PAR needs a variable of its own into which the handshake signal can be read. In constrast, the two branches do not need distinct copies of the message they are sending, since concurrent processes may read variables simultaneously without any difficulty.

The Merging Buffer

Re-writing the merging buffer is the most difficult part of creating a terminating pipeline. The difficulty arises because MergeBuf will receive termination commands on two input channels, and these may arrive at any time and in any order. Once such a command has been received, nothing else should be read from the channel on which it arrived, i.e. once a termination command arrives on a channel, that channel must be "turned off".

Programmers can place Boolean guards on ALT statements to give themselves this sort of control. In general, an ALT guard is of the form:

```
bool & chan ? data
```

where bool is some general Boolean expression, and chan ? data is some input process. This guard will be satisfied exactly when the Boolean evaluates to TRUE and the input process can proceed.

We start writing the new MergeBuf in the best of top-down styles:

```
PROC MergeBuf( CHAN OF pipeProt left, right, out )

  ...  variable declarations

  SEQ
    ...  initialise
    ...  loop
    ...  terminate
  :
```

The variable declarations include the buffer for the message, the loop controls, and two more Booleans for use as ALT guards:

```
--  variable declarations
INT msg.size :
[buffer.size]INT msg :
BOOL stop :
BOOL listening.to.left, listening.to.right:
```

The two Booleans listening.to.left and listening.to.right will act as guards on the channels from the left and right channels respectively. The initialisation section must set these to their starting values:

```
--  initialise
listening.to.left := TRUE
listening.to.right := TRUE
```

The loop section must operate as long as the process is supposed to forward messages from either of its inputs. This is true so long as either of the two Booleans initialised above is still true:

```
--  loop
WHILE (listening.to.left OR listening.to.right)
  ALT
    listening.to.left & left ? msg.size :: msg
      ...  deal with message from left

    listening.to.right & right ? msg.size :: msg
      ...  deal with message from right
```

Dealing with a message involves checking it to see whether it is a termination command, setting the appropriate Boolean to FALSE if it is or forwarding the message if it is not. For the left branch, this is:

```
  --  deal with message from left
SEQ
  testStopFlag( msg, stop )
  IF
    stop
      listening.to.left := FALSE
    TRUE
      out ! msg.size :: msg
```

The right branch is similar.

Once termination commands have been received on both input channels, the main loop will terminate and MergeBuf must forward a termination command to its output. This can be done by forwarding the last message received, since this message must itself have been a termination command:

```
  --  terminate
out ! msg.size :: msg
```

A Terminable N-Way Merging Buffer

A merging buffer capable of handling n input channels is only slightly more complicated than the process described in the previous section. Rather than testing the disjunction of the process's ALT guards to see whether any of the input channels are still active, this process, MergeBuf.n, keeps a count of the number of active input channels and only terminates when this number falls to zero. The whole process is:

```
PROC MergeBuf( []CHAN OF pipeProt in,
               CHAN OF pipeProt out )

  VAL n IS (SIZE in) :
  INT msg.size :
  [buffer.size]INT msg :
  BOOL stop :
  [n]BOOL listening :
  INT numListening :

  SEQ
    -- initialise controls
    numListening := n
    SEQ i =0 FOR n
      listening[i] := TRUE

    -- loop
    WHILE (numListening > 0)
      ALT i = 0 FOR n
        listening[i] & in[i] ? msg.size :: msg
          -- deal with message on channel i
          SEQ
            testStopFlag( msg, stop )
            IF
              stop
                SEQ
                  listening[i] := FALSE
                  numListening := numListening - 1
              TRUE
                out ! msg.size :: msg

    -- terminate
    out ! msg.size :: msg

  :
```

Putting It All Together

All of the processes described in this section have the same "shape", in
terms of input and output channels, as their predecessors. The same
MainNode and **EndNode** procedures used before can therefore be re-used,
as can the placement statement which put these processes on processors.

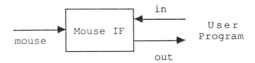

Figure 5.9: Mouse Interface Procedure

Once again, occam's modular approach to process design makes designing and modifying complex concurrent systems relatively simple.

5.2   A Mouse Interface

Not all transputers are used to build supercomputers. The transputer's ability to handle interrupts and communication swiftly and elegantly makes it ideal for use in embedded systems and real-time programming. This section shows how a typical application, a mouse interface, can be implemented in occam.

A good definition of a real-time system is one in which the program cannot delay its inputs. In the load-balancing pipeline described in the previous section, jobs were dealt with at the processors' speed – new jobs could enter the pipeline only as processors completed old jobs. In a real-time system, on the other hand, the rate at which new data enters the system is beyond the program's control.

A mouse interface is a typical real-time application for two reasons. First, the data being sent by the mouse arrives at a fixed rate. The interface procedure *must* deal with this data as it arrives; it cannot allow a back-log of data to pile up.

Second, many features of the mouse interface's design, such as the format in which the mouse's data arrives, are beyond the programmer's control. The interface must include code to transform raw data into a format which can be used by an applications program.

Application programs may go a long time without needing to know the mouse's position. Rather than inundate these programs with a continual stream of mouse updates, mouseIF uses a polling system. On one side of mouseIF is the channel mouse on which mouse data arrives. On the other side are two channels, in and out (Figure 5.9). When an program wants information from mouseIF it must send a single integer on in. mouseIF replies by sending three values on out: the changes in the mouse's X and

Y co-ordinates since the last query, and the current button status.

5.2.1 Reading Data from the Mouse

Mouse Data Format

The basic unit of information supplied by the mouse is a (dx,dy) change in mouse position. Between every two such records, the mouse supplies a status record showing which buttons are currently down. A whole mouse data record is therefore:

```
status; dx0; dy0; dx1; dy1
```

The mouse itself supplies these values as signed 8-bit integers. However, in order to be compatible with the rest of the operating system, each of these values is immediately put into the low byte of a 32-bit word. It is these 32-bit values which arrive on the `mouse` channel.

One other data value may also arrive on the `mouse` channel. Meiko's system code defines a special value, `endstreamch`, which is used to signal the end of input on a channel. Any procedure which reads data from the mouse channel must check to see if this value has been read, and, if it has, stop reading and set a flag to show that the mouse handler is to terminate. The way in which this is done will be seen below.

Synchronisation and the Status Word

One recurrent problem in real-time systems design is noise. For any number of reasons, the occasional byte of information from the mouse can be lost by the system. It is important that `mouseIF` be able to re-synchronise with the mouse when this happens.

The bits in the status word's low byte always takes the format:

```
10000LMR
```

where `LMR` represents three bits which are only 0 when the left, middle, or right buttons respectively are down. If interpreted as an integer, this bit pattern has a value of approximately -60; since the normal change in a mouse's X or Y coordinate between successive reports will be an order of magnitude less, it is possible to detect a status word by checking for the `10000xxx` pattern (where x means "don't care").

The procedure `getStatus` implements this check, as well as the check for `endstreamch`:

```
PROC getStatus(CHAN OF ANY mouse, INT status, BOOL running)

  SEQ
    WHILE ((status <> endstreamch) AND
           ((status /\ #F8) <> #80))
      mouse ? status
    IF
      status = endstreamch
        running := FALSE
      TRUE
        status := (BITNOT status) /\ #07
  :
```

(The notation #XX represents a hexadecimal integer.) For reasons explained below, getStatus assumes that the procedure calling it has already read a word from mouse. If this word contains the correct bit pattern, getStatus checks to see whether the word is an endstreamch. If it is, getStatus sets a termination flag as required. If it is not, getStatus masks out all but the low 3 bits of the word, which it then inverts. This leaves only the button status in the word, with 1's indicating buttons which are down. This inversion is done because a "1 for down" format is more convenient for application programs to use.

If getStatus encounters a word which does not have the correct bit pattern, it continues reading until a value with the appropriate pattern arrives. This means that the mouse interface may skip a complete data record in order to re-synchronise. However, since these records are arriving constantly, and each represents a relatively small increment in position, this does not cause any great harm. In other systems, the issues of noise and synchronisation may be important enough that they dominate the design.

Reading Changes in Position

Now that the button status word has been read, the two (dx,dy) pairs showing how the mouse has moved must be read:

```
PROC getAllDeltas(CHAN OF ANY mouse, [4]INT deltas,
                  BOOL running)

  INT i :
  SEQ
    i := 0
    WHILE (running AND (i < 4))
      SEQ
        getDelta(mouse, deltas[i], running)
        i := i + 1
:
```

getDelta is complicated by a need to check the incoming data for an endstreamch. If one is encountered, the running flag must be set to FALSE to stop the mouse interface.

Another complication in getDelta comes from the way mouse data is packed into integers. As mentioned above, the operating system puts each 8-bit integer of mouse data into the low byte of a 32-bit word. The sign bit of the 8-bit value is *not* extended when this is done. This means that if the 32-bit values coming in on mouse are used directly, they will have the wrong numeric value whenever the original 8-bit value was negative. Thus, getDelta must explicitly perform a sign-extend operation. This is done by testing the top bit of the original 8-bit value, and setting all bits above it to 1 if it is 1:

```
PROC getDelta(CHAN OF ANY mouse, INT delta, BOOL running)

  SEQ
    mouse ? delta
    IF
      (delta = endstreamch)
        running := FALSE
      (delta /\ #80) <> 0    -- original value negative
        delta := delta \/ (BITNOT #FF)   -- sign extend
      TRUE                   -- original value positive
        SKIP
:
```

5.2.2 Handling Interactions

Now that a pair of procedures for reading data from the mouse channel have been written, we must combine them within the procedure mouseIF which can co-ordinate mouse data and user requests. This procedure must take into account the way human beings press buttons.

The mouse being supported is a standard 3-button mouse. Many applications require users to press two or three buttons at the same time. Unfortunately, human reactions are sufficiently imprecise that it is very difficult to actually get both or all three button signals occurring together; there is normally a short (fraction of a second) lag between the buttons going down.

In order to deal with this, mouseIF will use a time window for collecting button presses. As these latter are colloquially known as "bops", this time window is commonly called a *bopping* window. When a mouse button goes down, the bopping window is started. While this window is active mouse data is still collected, but requests from the user are held pending. If no new button activity occurs within the window, the single button press which opened it is given to the user. If more buttons are pressed, on the other hand, the button status is updated and the bopping window re-started. Figure 5.10 shows how mouse data and user requests are coordinated by using bopping windows.

5.2.3   The Mouse Handler

In outline, the whole of mouseIF is a loop containing a prioritised ALT:

```
PROC mouseIF( CHAN OF INT mouse, in, out )

   ...   constant and variable declarations

 SEQ
   ...   initialisation
   WHILE running
     PRI ALT
        ...   mouse update
        ...   bop result
        ...   request from user
 :
```

The PRI ALT's three branches deal with arrival of data from the mouse, the end of a button-pressing time window, and requests from the application program. The way each of these is done is explained below.

First, what needs to be initialised ? mouseIF has a Boolean loop control, running; this must be set to TRUE. mouseIF must also keep track of the change in mouse position since the last user request, and the button status;

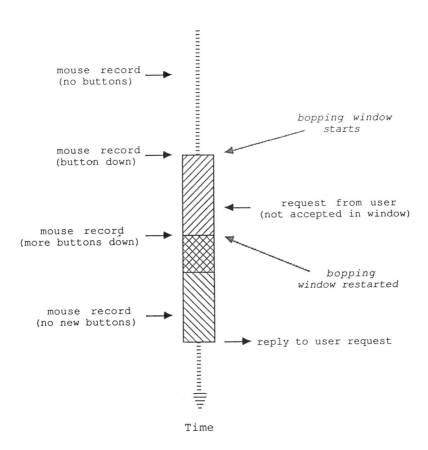

Figure 5.10: Interaction Using Bopping Windows

the variables recording each of these must be initialised to 0. Finally, a
Boolean control called bopping is used to indicate whether or not mouseIF
is within a bopping window. This condition is initially FALSE.

```
--  initialisation
running := TRUE
dx := 0
dy := 0
buttonStat := 0
bopping := FALSE
```

Servicing User Requests

mouseIF sends the most recent changes in mouse position and the current
button status to an application program only when that program requests
it to. This request takes the form of a single integer (the value of which is
ignored) arriving on in. Such requests are only serviced outwith a bopping
window. Once the request has been serviced, the button status and mouse
position change variables are zeroed so that the mouse interface may start
recording changes afresh:

```
--  request from user
(NOT bopping) & in ? any
  SEQ
    out ! dx; dy; buttonStat
    dx := 0
    dy := 0
    buttonStat := 0
```

Updates from the Mouse

When data arrives from the mouse, three things must be done:

1. the button status and (dx,dy) values must be read;

2. the change in mouse position since the last user request must be
   updated; and

3. if any new buttons have been pressed, the bopping window must be
   (re-)started.

```
--  mouse update
mouse ? newButtonStatus
  SEQ
    getStatus(mouse, newButtonStatus, running)
    getAllDeltas(mouse, deltas, running)
    ...  update dx, dy
    ...  reset timer if status has increased
```

The trigger on this ALT branch is the arrival of data from the mouse. The fact that this first word must be read to trigger the branch is the reason why getStatus takes a previously-read word as a parameter.

If the call to getStatus discovers that the value mouseButtonStatus read from the mouse channel was in fact an endstreamch, or if in the process of synchronising it hits an endstreamch, no more data will be coming from the channel. getAllDeltas includes complete tests on running for the end of the data stream to make sure that it does not try to read from a channel which has just been closed.

Once a set of values have been read, they must be used to update the mouse interface's current state. Updating the mouse's position is done by adding the two X values to dx, and the two Y values to dy. This addition is done using the modulo addition operator PLUS, rather than the normal +, so that if the user does not poll the mouse for a long time the repeated additions will not overflow. The possible side effects of this are dealt with by the clearMouse procedure described at the end of this section.

```
--  update dx, dy
dx := dx PLUS (dx0 + dx1)
dy := dy PLUS (dy0 + dy1)
```

Finally, if the user has pressed some more buttons since the last data record was read, the button status must be updated and the bopping window must be restarted. This latter operation is done by getting a new start-of-window time from the TIMER, and setting the bopping flag to TRUE:

```
--  reset timer if status has increased
IF
  buttonStat < newButtonStatus
    SEQ
      time ? t
      buttonStat := newButtonStatus
      bopping := TRUE
  TRUE
    SKIP
```

Using the "1 for down" convention produced by getStatus, the test

```
buttonStat < newButtonStatus
```

is satisfied only when more buttons are down in newButtonStatus than
were down in buttonStat.

Closing the Window

The last thing to do is to close up the bopping window after the delay
period has passed. This only needs to be done if mouseIF is currently in
such a window, so this ALT branch must be guarded in part by bopping.
The other part of the guard must be a delay after the value of t set by
the last mouse data to arrive. If mouseIF is in a bopping window, and the
time has expired, then bopping is set FALSE to show that the window has
closed:

```
--  bop result
bopping & time ? AFTER (t PLUS buttonWaitTime)
  bopping := FALSE
```

Tidying Up

Now that the procedure has been written, we can go back and fill in the
fold containing the procedure's variable declarations. The use of folds in
this way is not a part of the occam language, but is very good style, as it
makes the structure of programs and procedures much easier to read.

```
--  constant and variable declarations
BOOL running :
BOOL bopping :
VAL buttonWaitTime   IS ticksPerSecond / 5 :
TIMER time:
INT newButtonStatus :   -- bop just received
[4]INT deltas :
INT dx0 IS deltas[0] :
INT dy0 IS deltas[1] :
INT dx1 IS deltas[2] :
INT dy1 IS deltas[3] :
INT any :
INT dx, dy, buttonStat :
INT t :      -- time since last button status change
```

The constant ticksPerSecond is defined by the operating system. The
declaration

```
dx0 IS deltas[0] :
```

creates an alias `dx0` for the array element `deltas[0]`. The sparing use of
such aliases can make code easier to understand.

Why Use a PRI ALT?

`mouseIF` will not work properly if a normal `ALT` is used instead of a `PRI ALT`.
The reason for this is a phenomenon known as `livelock`.

Livelock is the inverse of the more common phenomenon of deadlock.
Deadlock occurs when two processes are trying to send to each other before
reading anything, as in:

```
CHAN OF INT A.to.B, B.to.A :
INT A.dat, B.dat :
PAR
  SEQ  -- process A
    A.to.B ! 0
    B.to.A ? A.dat
  SEQ  -- process B
    B.to.A ! 0
    A.to.B ? B.dat
```

Since neither process will read until the other has sent, but neither can send
until the other has read, the two processes lock up.

Livelock is a subtler plague. Consider what happens in the code segment
below if data is constantly arriving on both channels:

```
WHILE TRUE
  ALT
    chan1 ? x
      out ! x
    chan2 ? x
      out ! x
```

If both `chan1` and `chan2` are ready, a particular occam implementation
might always choose the same one – the choice between two ready channels
is arbitrary, which is not necessarily the same as random. If an implementation behaves this way, one or the other channel might be locked out,
never able to engage in communication. This situation is similar to that
of a secretary who is kept so busy answering the telephone that he has no
time to type letters.

A `PRI ALT` can be used in this procedure to avoid livelock, so long as
it is used carefully. When compared to a transputer's clock ticks, the rate

at which data arrives from a mouse is very slow. If requests from the
application program were given precedence in the PRI ALT over data from
the mouse, it is likely that there would be so constant a stream of them that
data coming from the mouse would never be read. (This situation occurred
during the testing of mouseIF, and took a considerable time to track down.)
The branch servicing the mouse channel must therefore always be the first
checked. An interface with its priorities wrong is not incorrect occam, but
exhibits incorrect behaviour.

5.2.4   User Interface Procedures

The last thing to do when writing an interface is to hide as many details
of the implementation as possible. In the case of mouseIF, there are two
things an application should not have to worry about: the exact format of
the data request, and the problem of mouse coordinate changes wrapping
around due to the use of PLUS. This last consideration is just a special case
of a more general problem – when an application requests its first set of
values from mouseIF, it has no way of knowing how long mouseIF has been
accumulating those values.

Two interface routines, getMouseData and clearMouseData, free the
user from having to worry about these problems. getMouseData handles
the mechanics of requesting values from mouseIF:

```
PROC getMouseData( CHAN OF INT toMouse, fromMouse,
                   INT dx, dy, button )

  SEQ
    toMouse ! 0  -- any value will do
    fromMouse ? dx; dy; button
  :
```

clearMouse clears the current state of the mouse by requesting values
from the mouse, which causes mouseIF to clear its internal state, and then
throws away the mouse interface's reply:

```
PROC clearMouse( CHAN OF INT toMouse, fromMouse )

  INT a, b, c :
  SEQ
    toMouse ! 0
    fromMouse ? a; b; c
  :
```

References

E. BARTON, *Data Concurrency and the Computing Surface*, Meiko Ltd., Bristol, 1987.

D. MAY and R. SHEPHERD *Communicating Process Computers*, INMOS Technical Note 22, Bristol, 1987.

Chapter 6

Parallel Architectures

6.1 Introduction

For many years the development of computers and the change in their architecture has been of relatively little importance to the user. This is understandable if the software produced by the user is readily transferred between different computers, especially between the user's current machine and a new machine. Software compatibility over this extended period has led to the development of large packages, which are the result of considerable investment. The challenge that faces us today is that posed by the VLSI technology revolution. The outstanding progress made in miniaturisation and micro-fabrication is initiating radical changes in computer design, and to capitalise on the increase in cost-effectiveness that this delivers, we are forced to reconsider our whole software strategy. Furthermore there are other technologies getting considerable support which may develop to a point where they are competing with Si and $GaAs$ VLSI, especially when the new software strategy is firmly in place.

It has been recognised for a long time that computation speed can be vastly improved by using parallelism; indeed this was recognised by Babbage well before the electronic computer was conceived. The earliest of these computers worked bit-serially, using a single central processor. Thus if two numbers were to be added together, the result was formed bit by bit. This mode of operation soon gave way to a form of parallelism, in which parts of the representative words were treated together, though the serial time-sequence of computational instructions was still operative. The user observed an increase in power from this innovation, compounded with the increase due to the advance of technology; users were not generally aware of the various reasons for the improved performance, but were satisfied as the old code ran quicker.

To sustain the advance in cost-effectiveness of computing, other aspects of parallelism were incorporated, leading to the development of the pipelined computers. In the execution of any arithmetic process there are a number of distinct stages, and these various stages can best be done using different specialised hardware. Therefore after the first stage of the arithmetic process has been completed the hardware concerned can be made available to start another independent process on new data. The various stages of the overall arithmetic processes thus overlap, better use is made of the hardware and a greater speed is attained on the problem being done. This progress has been achieved in the vector supercomputers without the need for new user software, but users have had to make certain minor changes, and the art of *vectorising* code is now widely practised. To be able to vectorise code successfully one has to know what tasks can be done independently, and therefore in parallel, but at this level there is not very much difficulty and all difficulties can be left unsolved by leaving the old code alone.

We have now reached the stage where any further real advance will entail rethinking our software. Parallelism must be exploited on a much more extensive scale in order to make use of the benefit of massive cheap replication of complex circuit chips. The density of components that can be integrated on to a chip is now so great that a single chip can perform all the electronic functions of a computer. The development costs of a successful chip are very large as compared with the cost of bulk production, and therefore any computer whose design consists of a massive number of identical chips will clearly be the cheapest to produce and to maintain, and if the design facilitates the building of machines of varying sizes, a most viable product will result. Computers are now being constructed with thousands of similar chips, interconnected in some way, and it is a considerable intellectual challenge to find the best way of making the interconnections and of using the resulting computer. Architecture now impinges on the avid user as it is the key to success with VLSI technology.

For the last seven years we have been aware of this impending technology revolution, and in 1979 the three avenues which seemed to us the most promising for large-scale computation were the Motorola 68000, the FPS 164 and the ICL DAP. The 68000 was arguably in essence the first 'computer on a chip' produced in bulk. At present the front-runner in this category is the transputer, its position of eminence depending in good measure on its communications ability. Multiply-connected FPS machines are the basis of IBM's ℓ-CAP, the logical progression being to FPS's T-series. Other companies have decided on concurrent use of much more powerful processors, such as the CRAY XMP and successors, the HEP (company now out of business), and ETA's GF-10. Hypercube connectivity (see later) now enjoys much attention and the requisite software is still developing. The architecture of the DAP has its restrictions, and an attempt to overcome them has led to the construction of the Connection Machine.

For a relative assessment of the available computers a number of aspects need to be considered:

- overall cost of the computer,

- maintenance cost,

- running cost, including personnel,

- availablity of system software,

- ease of programming,

- possibility of importing code.

We have recently engaged in benchmarking some front-runners as it is very difficult to get a reliable estimate of performance from manufacturer's specifications. Many manufacturers measure performance in MIPS (million instructions per second), a debatable measure of ability even for logic; Mflops (million floating point operations per second) is a standard measure for scientific computations, but may be misleading as an unattainable peak performance is usually quoted. Nevertheless we have learnt that a peak performance is *that which in no circumstances can be exceeded.*

Keeping up to date with the development of parallel computers is not an easy task, perhaps the best way to do it is to set up and stock a laboratory of these computers as Jack Dongarra has done at Argonne. We aim here to identify a number of computers to watch, and the details we give, especially of the paper computers, could readily become out of date. Undoubtedly there are omissions, such as the APE project, the IBM 3090, Convex, Cedar, to name but a few. We do not expect the VLSI technology to become out of date soon, but think it worthwhile to take a glimpse at what may become competing technologies in the distant future.

6.2 Basic Architectures

6.2.1 SIMD parallelism

A very simple way to construct a massively parallel computer is to connect processing elements (PEs) in a two-dimensional array, where each PE has four neighbouring PEs. The ICL DAP (see later) is the best example of

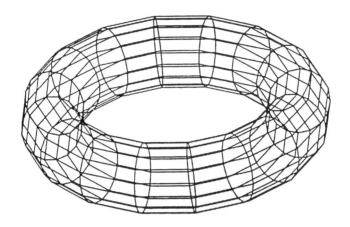

Figure 6.1: 16×16 processor torus

this construction available today. The mode of operation is SIMD (single instruction, multiple data-stream), in which the instructions of the program are broadcast to all the PEs simultaneously, whereupon each PE executes the instruction using the data set which is stored locally. Communications between the PEs are east/west or north/south on the array, and in the DAP the array can be taken to have either fixed or cyclic boundary geometry. On a DAP with 64×64 PEs, the longest communications path is 32 steps east/west followed by 32 steps north/south, involving 61 PEs which have no interest in the data received from one neighbour which it has to pass on to another neighbour.

The machine architecture of the DAP is often described as having its PEs on a torus. This can be understood from figure 6.1, drawn for a 16×16 DAP. The lines in this diagram can be thought of representing the connections between PEs, or alternatively the areas on the torus can be thought of as the PEs. It is clear from this figure that the longest path between processors does become rather large.

Some SIMD machines have eight neighbour connections, and others have a hypercube geometry. A fuller description is given later.

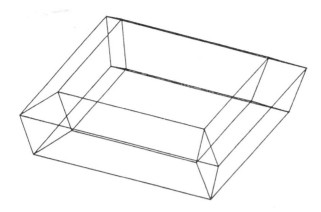

Figure 6.2: 4-D hypercube or 4×4 torus

6.2.2   Hypercube geometry

In an effort to reduce the number of processors which have to pass on information in which they have no direct interest, computer architects have turned their attention back to the binary hypercube construction as an interconnection scheme for multi-processor machines. For a machine of $N = 2^n$ processors, each processor is connected to n neighbours. Thus processor i has communication paths to all processors j such that the binary representations of i and j differ by 1 bit. The maximum data path length is n, a considerable saving over the two-dimensional mesh geometry. A diagrammatic representation of any hypercube beyond four dimensions becomes rather confusing, so a 4-dimensional example is chosen for figure 6.2. This is not in one of the forms often presented, but has been prepared by the same plotting program which produced figure 6.1. This is possible because the 4-dimensional hypercube is topologically equivalent to the 4×4 DAP, a coincidence that does not occur for higher dimensions.

A modified form of hypercube geometry is used in the SIMD Connection Machine (see later), but most of the machines with a true hypercube geometry are MIMD.

One aspect which is very important to consider in a large computer is *redundancy*. If one small part of the computer fails, does this mean that the whole computer should be inoperable? For the DAP or hypercube architecture this would seem to be the case (but see AMT DAP later), but it is possible to build in some redundancy to give a more robust machine. This

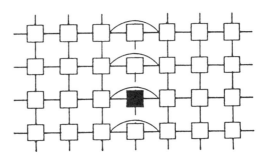

Figure 6.3: Short-circuit of a column of PEs

is possible by including an extra column of processors (actually 4 columns in the case of the MPP, see later) into the array, so that when one PE fails, say the black one in figure 6.3, the whole column can be short-circuited in software.

6.2.3 MIMD concurrency

The Multiple Instruction, Multiple Data-stream machine is the most general possible. It has become a feasible proposition over the last few years due to the cheapness of microprocessor systems. Numerous microprocessors can be linked together in a loosely-bound network in which they all have their own independent memory, or they can be combined as a tightly-bound multiprocessor in which each processor can access *any* memory. The program which runs on a MIMD machine is obeyed by all the processors, but each processor will be at a different place in the program at any one moment. In order to contrast with the parallelism of SIMD, the term *concurrency* is used in this context.

The range of MIMD computers can be roughly divided into those which are constructed out of (a) large processors each of which could be the basis of a powerful computer, (b) processors which occupy a board and which are equivalent to a full mini-computer, and (c) single-chip processors which can perform the full range of requisite functions. Our main interest is in category (c) where the single chip is the transputer, but the present chapter aims to touch upon the full range. The possibility of a category (d) in which there are many processors on a single chip is only viable at present with SIMD processing elements.

The architecture of computers in category (a) is often complicated in

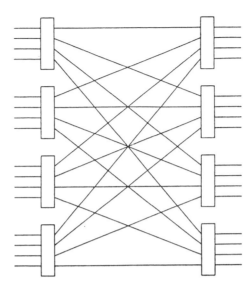

Figure 6.4: Butterfly switch

detail but simple in essence. The number of large, powerful units in any machine is never enormous, and so it is possible to have connectivity between any two units which need communications. For category (b) this is not the case, and a design decision must be made as to where to place the memory in relation to the processors. One common solution is typified by the BBN Butterfly (see later) in which there are memory units shared by the processors through a switch. This switch cannot be a crossbar as a crossbar gives direct communication between each processor and each memory unit. The switch shown in figure 6.4 has two rows of 4×4 crossbars and connects 16 processors on one side to 16 memory units on the other. This can be extended to a switch between 64 processors and 64 memory units by using a third row of 4×4 crossbars.

Although switch technology is improving to the point where the number of processors and memory units so connected can be in thousands, the fundamental architecture is not optimum for category (c). As miniaturisation continues to give a higher device density it becomes more practical to locate the memory much more closely to the processors. Of course this is an option for category (b) and is implemented in hypercube machines. The optimum machine architecture depends very often on the problem in hand, and it is for this reason that it is very attractive to have a machine where the topology can be designed by the user, as in the case of the Computing

Surface due to its reconfigurability. This freedom may well be the key to the successful exploitation of massively parallel computers.

6.2.4   Local or Global Memory ?

The question as to whether the memory in a highly parallel computer should be local to the processors or globally available is fundamental for the modern computer designer. The BBN Butterfly design is one where the processors access global memory through the switch, but each processor does have a cache of local memory, otherwise it would be using the switch repetitively for basic data.

The ICL DAP has its memory local with each processing element, but there is an efficient way for each processor to access global memory when needed through the broadcasting mechanism.

Thus there is no one clear answer; each computer is a compromise in this respect, although it is usually quite clear as to which category the particular computer is in.

6.3   Some Specific Computers

The following gives some information about a selection of machines in various categories. The list is by no means exhaustive.

6.3.1   SISD - pipeline processors

These are the computers most favoured for central facilities, such as the CRAY-XMP. In these computers, mathematical operations are pipelined and performed on data which flows through the processor in a stream. In the computers here described the data stream is a single vector stream so the operation mode is SISD. A great advantage of these machines is that old serial code can be run without modification, users then being able to improve performance by 'vectorising' the costly sections of code. This is what makes them ideal for a large community, especially as they are more cost-effective when vectorised than the ubiquitous VAX which we do not consider here. The running costs of these computers is high as the power consumption is a large fraction of a Mwatt, much of this being used in cooling. The complexity of such a facility is demanding in maintenance staff, and an extensive operation staff is needed as for any general purpose computer.

There are computers which compare very favourably with those presented in the following three short sections, and have the advantages that go with smaller size. The most notable is the FPS 264. Although omitted here, it should not be passed over when searching for the best general purpose computer of this architecture.

CRAY XMP, CRAY-2, CRAY-3

The XMP (eXperimental Multi-Processor), introduced in 1982, is available with 1, 2 or 4 processors. Each processor has a 9.5ns clock and has a peak performance of 400 Mflops. The 4 processor version has 64 Mbytes of memory. Also available is a solid-state storage device (SSD) with memory sizes up to 8 Gbytes, and a new disk drive (DD-49) which has 1.2 Gbytes capacity and 10 Mbyte/s bandwidth. Transfer to and from the SSD is via one or two 1 Gbyte/s channels. The prototype XMP/48 can achieve a 3.8 speed-up and so reach the Gflops range. The cost of a 4 processor XMP is around $20M which, at 50% peak, should deliver 0.8 Gflops. The design owed a lot to Steve Chen, who has recently left Cray Research to found a new company, Supercomputer Systems, which may well further the development of this computer architecture.

The multi-processor CRAY-2 has a new vector register architecture and uses liquid-immersion to obtain a 4ns clock. It is about as powerful as the XMP but has a much larger memory. The CRAY-3 is a *GaAs* version of the CRAY-2, being developed for the 1990s. It will be one cubic foot in size, have 16 processors with 2ns clock and memory twice as fast as that in the CRAY-2, giving a speed-up over this computer by a factor of 8.

CYBER-205, ETA GF-10

The CDC CYBER-205 evolved from the STAR-100. It is available with 2 or 4 general purpose pipelines, a 20ns clock and up to 128 Mbytes memory with 80ns access time. It is highly competitive with the CRAY-1, being faster for large vectors but slower for small vectors. A re-engineered 2-pipe CYBER-205 is the processor for the GF-10, constructed with 8 such processors by the CDC-funded Engineering Technology Associates company. Each VLSI CMOS processor should run about 3 times faster than the CYBER-205, having a 5ns clock and 256 Mbytes local memory. The whole computer, occupying a 5 foot cube cooled by liquid nitrogen, will have a further 2 Gbytes of shared memory. The GF-10 peak performance is 10 Gflops, but there is a version of the computer with a considerably slower performance which utilises the same chips but at room temperature; it appears that a good fraction of the chips do not function at low temperatures at the specification required for the main machine, but perform well at slower speeds at room temperature.

Facom VP, Hitac S-810, NEC SX and MITI's plans

The three largest Japanese computer companies have been developing computers comparable with the CRAY and CYBER series. A detailed comparison is out of place here. Fujitsu's Facom VP-100 and VP-200 peak at 250 and 500 Mflops, Hitachi's Hitac S-810/10 and /20 are marginally faster at 315 and 630 Mflops, the most powerful being NEC's SX-1 and SX-2 at 570 and 1300 Mflops. These three companies, in collaboration with Oki, Toshiba and Mitsubishi, are currently involved in MITI's (Japanese Ministry of International Trade and Industry) National Super-Speed Computer Project. This is a five year programme of R&D aimed at producing a 10 Gflops computer system with 1 Gbyte of semiconductor memory and 100 Gbytes of disk storage by March 1990.

6.3.2 SIMD - processor arrays

These computers are constructed as described above; arrays of identical processing elements (PEs) operating in lockstep and performing the same operation on different data.

Distributed Array Processor, DAP

The DAP, made by International Computers Limited, was begun in 1972 and the first production machine was installed in 1980 at Queen Mary College, London. It comprises a 64×64 array of PEs, each with 4 Kbits of associated memory (16 Kbits now at QMC), and is a memory module of a 2900 ICL mainframe which acts as a host. The PEs are two-dimensionally connected to the four nearest neighbours on a torus, and access highways to them, along the two dimensions, contribute greatly to the DAP's performance. Each PE can only perform bit-serial arithmetic, so arithmetic operations must be done in software offering a word-length flexibility unavailable in conventional computers. The first generation DAP is SSI/MSI with 16 PEs and their memory per circuit board. So the whole array takes 256 boards and occupies eight cabinets. The clock is 250ns including memory access. The machine is air cooled and consumes 25KW power.

Programming of the DAP is done in a version of Fortran, now called Fortran-plus, the host machine using standard Fortran. Effort is therefore needed in software conversion. Our experience in using this machine, in work that has produced nearly 200 scientific publications, is that it is easy to program and that it runs at around 20 Mflops on most problems. However there are certain problems for which it is not well suited, mainly those where there is a need to have a continually changing mapping of a problem on to the computer architecture. These difficulties may be less severe on a machine with considerably more memory, as new algorithms may then be used. For problems where reduced word-length operations are appropriate, especially boolean logic, the machine is extremely fast.

AMT DAP family

The third generation DAP, for which the ICL mil-DAP is the second generation and the prototype, is made by a new company, Active Memory Technology (Reading, UK and Irvine, California). A 32×32 array of bit-serial LSI/VLSI PEs with a 80-100ns clock forms the DAP 510, which can be hosted on a MicroVAX or a Sun workstation. Each PE chip contains 64 PEs, and the 16 chips of a DAP 510 are duplicated by another set, giving extensive redundancy. Both PE sets work on the same data store, and the results of calculation are compared continuously. When there is disagreement, the faulty PE is ascertained and the computer is then run on the good set of PEs, giving the maintenance engineer time to make repairs at leisure.

The thinking behind the choice of number in the machine name, such as the DAP 510, suggests that a range of DAPs is contemplated. 5 is the power of 2 which gives 32 for the 32×32 machine, and 10 is the clock frequency, 10 MHz. A particular feature of this range of machines is the ability to run a colour graphics screen at about 70 Mbytes/s, very attractive for interactive work.

As the AMT DAP is hosted in a fashion very similar to the Meiko Computing Surface, there is surely great potential for building MIMD machines of heterogeneous architecture containing MIMD and SIMD processors. This is becoming even more important because the Connection Machine is creating a US market for SIMD technology and DEC has recently announced a 32-processor chip.

Connection Machine

This SIMD machine is made by Thinking Machines Corporation, Cambridge, Massachusetts. There are 16 bit-serial PEs on a chip, 32 chips to a board which contains 4 Kbits of memory per PE as in the DAP. Communications between the PEs on a single chip is very rapid, and we can consider each PE to be directly connected to the others on its chip. The chips are arranged as a 10 or 12 dimensional binary hypercube, giving a computer of 16384 or 65536 PEs. Routing through the hypercube gives this machine its flexibility, a very powerful feature, though the fact that the machine is not a full 14 or 16 dimensional binary hypercube sometimes causes communication delays. This can be understood by remembering that for a true binary hypercube of $65536 = 2^{16}$ PEs, each should be connected with 16 links, 12 of which should be off-chip. This would mean that there should be 16 links between any one chip and each of its hypercube neighbours, whereas there is only one such link, giving a severe constriction between the first four dimensions (on-chip) and the remaining twelve dimensions. Software exists to enable each PE to behave as an array of virtual PEs depending on the amount of memory available. TM are well aware of the need for more memory and for a basic chip upgrade. The CM is now programmed in *Lisp and in a parallel version of C.

The machine just described has been named the CM-1, as there is now a new version of the machine, the CM-2, which gives a more impressive performance. The performance of the CM-1 was roughly comparable to that of the ICL DAP, but the CM-2 now incorporates the power of the Wietek chip-sets. Each pair of processor chips has an attached Wietek, which means that at any moment when arithmetic is to be performed, there are 32 identical arithmetic tasks, one from each PE. These 32 tasks can then be pipelined into the Wietek. The 65536 PE machine therefore has 2048 Wieteks, and if these can be fed at their peak rate the machine would be delivering over 20 Gflops. Although only a small fraction of this is actually achieved, the machine is now very powerful, and as its present limitations are now in its communications ability we can expect TM to be putting considerable effort into improvement in this area. In many ways a comparison with IBM's GF-11 would be fruitful.

Massively Parallel Processor, MPP

Made in VLSI by Goodyear Aerospace Corporation, this SIMD computer has 132×128 bit-serial PEs (132=128+4, the 4 giving built-in redundancy) each with 1 Kbit memory. The high level language chosen for this machine is parallel Pascal. The power is projected to be 200 Mflops, but we have not been able to test this. The MPP was designed for NASA, and had problems in meeting specifications, which were perhaps a little unrealistic. A working machine has been constructed, but it is unlikely to become a commercial machine.

Cellular Logic Image Processor, CLIP

The pilot model (CLIP3) was built in University College, London, in 1973 and then the CLIP4 system in 1979. This is a 96×96 array of PEs each with 32bits of memory and connections to the eight nearest neighbours. The four-phase clock cycle is 400ns. It is used for image processing and pattern recognition. It has been redesigned with custom chips as CLIP7, a

4×512 array of PEs, each with 32 Kbits of memory, running with a 200ns clock. The programming language is an extension of C. This is now a company product of Stonefield Ltd. of Swindon, UK.

Adaptive Array Processor

The Japanese Nippon Telegraph and Telephone Public Corporation (NTT) is building an LSI Adaptive Array Processor. The prototype will use 128×128 2μ Si-gate p-well CMOS LSI chips, each chip containing an 8×8 PE array with peripheral circuits and each PE having a 96-bit memory. There will be an eight-nearest-neighbour PE connection network with hierarchical bypasses, allowing various types of two-dimensional data processing. The clock cycle will be 55ns, and power consumption 1.1W per chip.

The GEC GRID

The General Electric Company (UK) is building the GEC Rectangular Image and Data processor. It is to be a 64×64 PE array with each PE having 64bits of on-chip (register) memory and 64 Kbits of off-chip (main) memory, and being connected to its eight nearest neighbours. This arrangement probably gives the best of both worlds: a simple PE with a small fast 'cache' memory (as in CLIP and AAP) backed up by a large amount of slower memory (as in DAP, CM and MPP). The 64×64 array is to be made up of 16 boards each containing 2^4 GRID chips and their off-chip memory, each chip containing an 8×4 array of PEs and their associated on-chip memory, an edge control register, a histogram counter and the peripheral circuitry for instruction decoding and zero detection. The on-chip edge control register defines the PEs which form the edge of the array, thereby allowing the array to be connected in a variety of topologies: linear, cylindrical or toroidal. A minicomputer will host the GRID, running UNIX and using an extended C. Responsibility for the project has now been transferred to Marconi.

6.3.3 MIMD - multi-processors

BBN Butterfly

Bolt, Beranek and Newman (BBN) have developed the Butterfly Parallel Processor which is an MIMD tightly-coupled, shared-memory machine consisting of up to 256 68000 microprocessors, each with 1 to 4 Mbytes of memory, interconnected via a Butterfly switch. The single-board processors can be upgraded to 68020/68881 which yield 0.4 Mflops each. The Butterfly switch, which uses packet switching (see figure 6.4), is made up from 4×4 switching elements implemented as custom VLSI chips with 8 on a board forming a 16×16 switch. Machines with more than 16 processors have redundant paths. Interprocessor data transfers occur at 32 Mbyte/s and remote access is claimed to take less than 4 microseconds. The developments that BBN were making towards a computer they called the Monarch have been incorporated as improvements to the Butterfly, now called the GP1000. Other products should become available in 1988.

We have recently benchmarked the Butterfly, using molecular dynamics as the application. Calculations for each individual molecule are performed independently on the various processors, and we found that there was very good performance when the number of molecules exceeded the number of processors by a factor of 10 or more. Smaller ratios give rise to an increased computation loss due to contention in the switch. To make a general conclusion from this requires the knowledge that each molecule interacts with roughly 12 neighbours, and the quantity of data needed to calculate an interaction.

The Heterogeneous Element Processor

Denelcor of Denver, Colorado manufactured the MIMD Heterogeneous Element Processor which consists of up to 16 process execution modules (PEMs), each with its own data memory bank, connected to a switch. Each PEM can access its own data memory bank directly, but access to the other memories is through the switch. A PEM may run up to 64 processes concurrently. The switch is a high-speed, packet-switched network. Process synchronisation is achieved in hardware by the use of so-called asynchronous variables; they cannot be read from until they are full or written to until they are empty. Although Denelcor are now out of business, HEPs are still available for purchase.

The IBM ℓ-CAP

The Loosely Coupled Array of Processors has been built by Professor Enrico Clementi at IBM Kingston. This distributed system consists of 10 FPS-164 attached array processors hosted by an IBM 3081 with a peak performance of 110 Mflops, increasing to 550 Mflops by the addition of 2 **FPS MAX** boards to each processor. IBM have expressed a willingness to market this product, ℓ-CAP-1, and have installed a similar system at IBM Rome. ℓ-CAP-2 now exists at Kingston and has 10 FPS-264s hosted by an IBM 3084, peak performance being 330 Mflops.

The Ultracomputer and the RP3

New York University's Ultracomputer is a MIMD shared-memory machine in which the processors and memories are separate, but are interconnected through an Omega switching network. This switch is such that each processor is at the top of a binary tree whose leaves are the memories and vice versa. It is pipelined and packet-switched. An 8 processor prototype was built and a 4096 68000 processor version was planned to yield a 10 Gflops machine.

Many of the features of the Utracomputer project have now appeared in the IBM RP3 (Research Parallel Processing Project) and the first machine is to have 64 IBM 32bit microprocessors, 2 Gbytes of memory and a VLSI omega switch giving a possible 100 Mflops in 1988. This is to be followed by a 512 node version. The machine was to have combined two separate switch technologies, but it now appears that one of these technologies is thought to be sufficient. IBM state that this is not intended as a commercial product, though it clearly has potential as a rival to the Butterfly.

Myrias 512

The Myrias Research Corporation's first design, the Myrias 4000 distributed memory MIMD system was designed with configurations of up to 64K processors (measured as 64 Krates where 1 Krate = 1024 processors), giving an average performance of around 1.6 Gflops (32bit arithmetic). The minimum primary memory is 8 Gbytes, upgradeable to 32 Gbytes. The processors each consist of a 68000, 128 Kbytes 150ns dRAM and a high speed DMA interface. 8 processors together form a board, 16 boards populate a cage, 8 cages are housed in 1 Krate, 4 Krates form the minimum configuration - a 64×64 array with 512 Mbytes of memory. They also have 1 Gbyte disk storage and I/O bandwidth of 80 Mbyte/s per Krate. System is expandable in 1 Krate increments. An optical communications system is a feature of this machine, but it is not clear whether this will overcome the communications problem better than standard electronic links.

The modern machine, the Myrias 512 (due before 1989), has increased processing power due to the Motorola 68020 chips. Memory is also increased with 4 Mbytes dRAM per processor. It is hard to ascertain the exact nature of the machine architecture, though the company will willingly supply details as to how to write software for the machine. The languages supported are to be versions of Fortran and C, and will involve a simple extension which they call "par do" for parallel loops.

Caltech hypercube

Geoffrey Fox and Charles Seitz of the California Institute of Technology
designed the Caltech Hypercube comprising an array of microprocessors
with local independent memories. Nearest-neighbour connections are implemented by means of mailbox communications which operate as follows:
a processor waits on a mailbox until the data is put in by the neighbour,
and a processor waits on a mailbox until it becomes empty if it wishes to
deliver data to it. The processors are configured as a binary hypercube.

The first machine (after a four node prototype), which was completed
in October 1983 and called the Mark I Hypercube, has 64 nodes, each
of which is an Intel 8086/87 microprocessor with 128 Kbytes of memory
on a single board, giving a total of 3.2 Mflops. The Mark II Hypercube
(completed in September 1984) is as Mark I but with 256 Kbytes of memory.
It exists as one 128-node or four 32-node machines, and has an Intel 310
workstation as intermediate host. The present Mark III Hypercube is to be
firstly 32 then 256 and finally up to 1024 nodes, each of which contains a
Motorola 68020/68881 as main processor, another 68020 as I/O processor
plus Weitek scalar floating point chips (1064 multiplier and 1065 ALU - 12
Mflops for 32bit operation) and 4 Mbytes of memory. DMA will be used
as the communication method for message passing.

Subsequent to the work of Fox and Seitz there has been a marked increase in interest in binary hypercubes in USA. The machines described
in the following four subsections are indebted to this work, as also is the
Connection Machine, a SIMD version.

The FPS T-series

The T-series are homogeneous parallel computers with a modular structure
based on hypercube geometry, so that a wide range of system sizes is potentially possible. The basic unit is the module, or T-10, consisting of eight
node boards connected together as a 3-dimensional cube, a system board
and a disk. The system board is connected to each of the node boards
via a linear chain, to the disk, and to a front end computer which is a
MicroVAX running VMS. This system network is distinct from the hypercube interconnections between nodes. Additional communication links on
the system and node boards allow modules to be connected together; the
system boards are connected in a ring, the node boards are connected into
an n-dimensional hypercube (hypercube) where $n < 14$. The most common
configuration at present is the T-20, which forms a single cabinet, consisting of two modules in which the 16 nodes are connected as a 4-dimensional
hypercube; the T-100 consists of four cabinets in which the 64 nodes are

connected as a 6-dimensional hypercube (T-numbers represent the number of nodes in octal).

Each node board is a powerful vector computer in its own right, with a peak 64-bit performance of 16 Mflops. The original node design involved a Weitek coprocessor chip-set fed from 1Mbyte of video RAM controlled by a transputer (originally T414), the transputer being also responsible for communications. Potential (peak) performance ranged from 256 Mflops to 60 Gflops or more, depending on the number of nodes.

Although FPS are facing serious problems with the T-series, there is still progress being made as evidenced by the paper by Carlisle and Miles at the 3rd Conference on Hypercube Concurrent Computers, "Structured Asynchronous Communication Routines for the FPS T Series". This enables a complete development environment for Fortran programmers so that one program may control all the processors.

Intel's personal supercomputers, iPSC & iPSC-VX

The iPSC/d5 (d6 or d7) system contains 32, (64 or 128) nodes hosted by an Intel 310 workstation. Each node consists of a 80286/80287 microprocessor with 512 Kbytes of memory and 7 bidirectional channels (each giving 10 Mbit/s data transfer).

The iPSC-VX is Intel's machine in competition with the FPS T-series. It is a hypercube built from their 80286 and 80287 processors but with vector processors at each node. The ALU is pipelined with a 100ns clock and 1 Mbyte of 250ns dynamic RAM plus 16 Kbytes of 100ns static RAM. For 32bit arithmetic each node is theoretically capable of 20 Mflops. The communications capability of this machine left a lot to be desired, but Intel have recently improved this beyond recognition so that the machine now appears little different from a fully cross-barred machine. If this machine, the PSC/2, lives up to its specification it could well become the leading hypercube.

Ametek System 14

A hypercube is formed of from 16 to 256 nodes and is connected to any VAX (running Unix or VMS) as a host via a 1 Mbyte/s parallel interface. Each node consists of a 80286/80287 microprocessor and 1 Mbyte of memory with 8 bidirectional channels (each 3 Mbyte/s). It runs the Ametek Hypernet Operating System (HOS), as will the Caltech Mark III Hypercube. First machines were projected for early 1986 costing about $100K for 32 nodes.

NCUBE

One to four boards, each containing 4 processors, form the 8 Mflops NCUBE/four which has an IBM PC-AT bus interface; 1 to 16 boards, each containing 64 processors, form the 500 Mflops NCUBE/ten. Each processor consists of an NCUBE custom VLSI chip which contains a 32-bit processor, a 16-bit error correcting memory interface (to 128 Kbytes of memory) and 22 independent DMA communication links (11 in and 11 out) with a claimed data transfer rate of 1 Mbyte/s. One pair of links is used for system I/O. There are eight 90 Mbyte/s system I/O channels - one for each set of 128 nodes connected via I/O boards. One of the I/O boards is a host board containing an 80286/80287 with 4 Mbytes of memory which runs a Unix style operating system called Axis, supporting 8 users and facilitating allocation of subsets of the hypercube. (Each node runs a simple operating system called Vertex.) The other I/O boards may do other things such as graphics.

The NCUBE chip is the closest single chip to compare with the Inmos transputer, but the company do not appear to be marketing the chip independently from its computer. Although it has 11 links as compared with the transputer's four, the total bandwidth for communications is comparable but somewhat less than for the T800 transputer.

Suprenum

The Suprenum computer is being constructed in Germany by Suprenum GmbH, supported by the Gesellschaft fur Mathematik und Datenverarbeitung. It is a MIMD computer made of processors arranged on a grid of clusters as shown on figure 6.5 This diagram shows the 256-node prototype where, associated with each cluster of 16 processors there is a disk unit. The processors are connected by a two-level system of very fast buses, and it appears that advantage will be taken of the grid structure of one of these buses for suitable applications. This is being talked of as part of a European supercomputer, though the hardware will not be indigenous.

IBM's GF-11

This machine was to have been called the GF-10, but ETA just got there first. It has been in design and construction for some years, and is expected to be in operation before the end of 1988. It is not intended as a commercial product, rather as a highly efficient machine for a restricted purpose known to physicists as QCD. We include it here as it shares a distinction with the CM-2 as being a very large assembly of Wietek chip-sets. It is designed as MIMD, but will be used extensively in a SIMD mode due to the nature

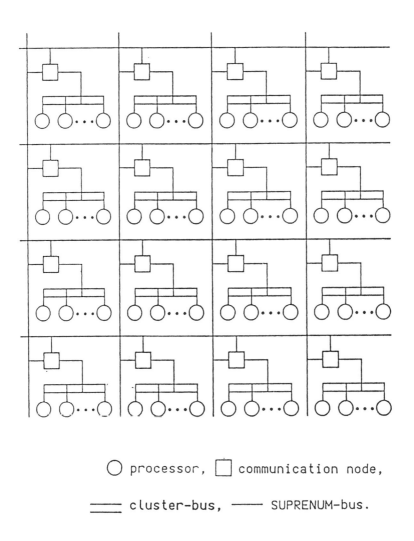

○ processor, ☐ communication node,

═══ cluster-bus, ─── SUPRENUM-bus.

Figure 6.5· Architecture of the 256-node Suprenum.

of the particular problem for which it was designed. It is based on 24×24
crossbars, giving a full configuration of 576 processors, with extra processors
for redundancy reasons. The original design probably had one Wietek per
processor, but now there will be two. The name GF-11 was chosen as the
peak performance of this quantity of Wieteks is about 11 Gflops, and again,
due to the nature of QCD, this peak may well be often achieved. We believe
the delays of recent months have been due, not to design reasons but due
to the difficulties of construction.

Sequent BALANCE and Alliant FX-series

A number of multi-processor systems have recently appeared which aim
to provide improved performance through concurrency, in a way which is
essentially transparent to the user. This is typically achieved by tightly-
coupled processors sharing common memory. Examples are the Sequent
BALANCE and the Alliant FX-series. As yet such machines have a modest
number of processors, roughly up to 20, but are expected to achieve very
high performance with future upgrades.

Data-flow and systolic architectures

Computers of these architectures do not appear to be competitive for large-
scale scientific computing. Nevertheless this field of development must be
monitored especially as Japan's Electrotechnical Laboratory (ETL) is developing a large dataflow computer called SIGMA-1 which contains 256
PEs and should achieve 100 Mflops.

6.3.4   Transputer-based systems

The INMOS T414 transputer is a 1.5 μ CMOS VLSI chip which contains
a 10 MIPS, 32-bit RISC processor, 2 Kbytes of on-chip 50ns static RAM
and four 20 Mbit/s bidirectional communication links. It can address up to
4 Gbytes of off-chip memory with a bandwidth of 25 Mbyte/s. The RISC
architecture allows context switching to be very fast, supporting efficient
implementation of concurrent program execution on a single transputer.
The INMOS links support communications between programs running on
separate transputers. The serial protocol requires only two wires per link
in each direction, the respective pins of one transputer being directly connected to those of another. The point-to-point communication links allow
transputer networks of arbitrary size to be constructed, with the advantage
that the communications bandwidth does not saturate as the size of the
system increases. Each transputer in a system uses its own local memory.

Overall memory bandwidth is proportional to the number of transputers in the system, in contrast to a large global memory, where the use of additional processors tends to degrade memory bandwidth.

The transputer is designed to implement the process model of concurrency, expressed through the occam programming language, which was developed in parallel with the hardware. Communication between parallel processes is effected by uni-directional channels, which may connect processes on the same processor or on different processors. Each INMOS link implements two such channels, one in each direction. The transputer can be programmed in other high level languages such as Fortran, but that if concurrency is to be exploited, occam should be used as a harness to link modules written in the selected language.

The T212 Transputer is a 16-bit transputer providing up to 10 MIPS processing power with 2 Kbytes of on-chip RAM and four 20 Mbit/s links. The memory interface provides 64 Kbytes of direct address space with a maximum data rate of 20 Mbyte/s.

The most interesting member of the transputer family from the viewpoint of large-scale scientific simulations is the floating-point version of the transputer, the T800, with an integral hardware 64-bit floating point unit capable of 1.5 Mflops. It has 4 Kbytes of on-chip RAM for 80 Mbyte/s data rate, four 20 Mbit/s INMOS links, and an external memory interface with bandwidth of 26.6 Mbyte/s. The floating point unit has been designed to operate on both single-length (32 bit) and double-length (64 bit) floating point numbers to the ANSI-IEEE floating point standard. The T800 is claimed to achieve more than five times the performance of the Motorola MC68020/MC68881 combination on the Whetstone benchmark.

INMOS Transputer Evaluation Module

INMOS offer a wide range of boards and motherboard systems. Coupled to an IBM PC, or to a VAX, the result is an evaluation tool which is very useful for familiarisation and occam program development and constitutes a powerful computing device.

The Esprit 1085 Project

The development of the T800 floating point transputer has been partially funded through an Esprit project which involves RSRE, Thorn-EMI and Southampton University in the UK in addition to Inmos and European collaborators. This is the basis of a machine, the Reconfigurable Transputer Processor, comprising multiple supernodes, each constructed from 16 transputers interconnected by electronic switching. The machine is marketed in

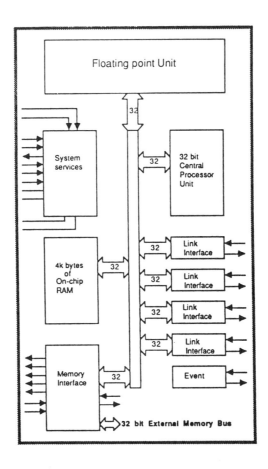

Figure 6.6: The T800 floating point transputer

the U.K. as the PARSYS SN1000.

ALICE

The Applicative Language Idealised Computing Engine is a highly parallel computer being designed and built at Imperial College out of 16 or 64 transputers. It is primarily for the parallel evaluation of declarative languages by graph reduction - hence it is termed a reduction machine. Declarative languages are languages with no assignment, so no side-effects, and no state (program history). They come in two varieties: functional (or applicative) and relational (or logic). Functional language programs comprise a set of data declarations, a set of functions to be performed on the data and a top-level expression whose evaluation produces the result of executing the program. Relational language programs comprise a set of assertions (facts), a set of rules and a query whose satisfaction is the result of the program.

The Meiko Computing Surface

The Computing Surface is a computer system designed by Meiko Ltd. of Bristol to exploit the power of the transputer on compute-intensive applications. Compute, graphics and I/O elements are available, together with interface and intermodule boards. The links from each element are electronically switched enabling the user to create the topology required by their program.

Physically, a Computing Surface is contained in one or more modules, which may be populated with a mixture of elements chosen according to the requirements of the user. In addition to each of its links, each processor has an interface to a supervisory mechanism. It is used for system services, error detection and forwarding debugging messages. The supervisor bus is controlled by the host processor in each module.

The compute elements are built from T414's or T800's each with between 256K and 48 MBytes of memory. A board carries up to 4 elements together with the network and supervisor bus interfaces.

Graphics boards supply 1.5MBytes of video ram, together with colour lookup tables and a screen refresh engine. They can be linked together (via a 200 MBytes/sec pixel bus) to extend the video ram and increase the graphics bandwidth.

A transputer with SCSI disk/peripheral interface and 8 MBytes of memory acts as a controller for disk and archiver systems. Many such systems can be joined to build a parallel disk I/O system.

The data port elements provide an interface between high bandwidth devices such as video cameras and multiple transputer memories/links enabling data to be scattered/broadcast amongst the processors at up to 80 MBytes/sec.

Meiko provide system software to control a Computing Surface in single or multi user mode, and are developing MEIKOS, a system V compatible UNIX[1] operating system.

The single user software (MDS) is a customised occam programming system. It has been modified for the Computing Surface and provides a UNIX style file structure. The multi-user software (MMVCS) implements a user-server system in which users (running UNIX kernels or OPS seats) make requests of servers (including fileservers and network interfaces) across a network. This network (the CSN) carries all their I/O traffic and protects them from each other.

There are compilers for Occam, C, Fortran and Pascal; each generate code for T414's and T800's. Communication over occam-style channels has been added to the conventional languages. Multiprocessor programs are built by linking sequential single processor programs (in C or Fortran) with an occam harness. Direct support is provided for simple models of parallel programming such as task farming.

Parsytec Megaframe Supercluster

The Supercluster is offered in two versions - the 64 and 256 with, respectively, 64 and 256 Inmos T800 processors. The transputers are grouped in clusters of 16 and linked through a network configuration unit. Each cluster has a pair of 16-channel communications lines. The clusters, in turn, are grouped in units of four, linked through two network-configuration units, to make the basic 64-processor Supercluster. However, unlike the Meiko Computing Surface, the Supercluster architecture does not have a global communications bus independent of the transputer links.

The NiCHE NT1000

The NT1000 is a system motherboard which plugs directly into the Sun-3 or Sun-4 VME bus, offering a range of I/O interfaces, plus sites for up to 32 computing modules. Each module consists of a T800 transputer combined with up to 10 Mbytes of fast local memory.

---

[1]UNIX is trademark of AT & T

6.4 New Technologies

6.4.1 Superconductor computers

A full range of devices for the construction of computers using the properties of superconductors has been developed, though in recent years interest has momentarily waned. The problems faced in using this technology are considerable, but the advantages of low power and high switching speeds are enormous; the switching times for superconducting devices can be as short as 5ps, and power consumption as little as 3 μW. A severe problem has been that superconducting devices have, until recently, needed the very low temperatures of liquid helium in order to function. Technological problems always increase dramatically when the temperatures involved are below the freezing point of air, but these difficulties may now be circumvented by the use of high-temperature superconductors.

A number of materials have recently been discovered which are superconducting at a temperature well above that required to liquefy air or nitrogen, and there is undoubtedly effort being put into developing the manufacturing processes by which these materials can be reliably made with sufficient purity. Although there is the glamorous prospect of room-temperature superconductivity, this is not nearly as important for computer technology as the ability to fabricate in VLSI. Single crystal perfection is one of the limiting factors in the progress of silicon implementation, and it is obviously going to be far more difficult for the new high-temperature superconducting materials which typically are a combination of at least four elements (e.g. yttrium barium copper oxide) rather than just one. The impact of this new technology is therefore not likely to be in this century, but when an impact is made it will surely be in the form of massively parallel devices, as the low power consumption will favour a very high device concentration.

The devices themselves are rather complex. They are based on the Josephson junction, a junction of insulating material between two superconductiong regions. In the superconductor, some of the electrons order in pairs, known as Cooper pairs, and these carry the current which experiences no resistance. Even without the application of an electric field to the Josephson junction, a current flows by a tunnelling (quantum-mechanical) mechanism across the junction. A junction with a current flowing represents one of the binary states required of a digital computer component. The other state is when the current is effectively switched off by introducing a control current which generates a magnetic field whose presence then causes the current through the device to be greater than the critical superconducting current, resulting in the loss of superconduction. This indirect control through the local magnetic field clearly means that the device mechanism is complex, a complexity which is further increased by the fact that the device latches onto the latter state even when the controlling current is removed. Thus by applying the control current the current through the junction is diverted to another route in the circuit, and stays in this route when the control current is removed, only returning to flow through the junction after being itself set briefly to zero. The latching problem can be overcome by setting all the junction currents in the computer regularly to zero, and to achieve this the whole computer is run with alternating current whose frequency determines (half) the machine's clock speed.

The Josephson junction technology has been developed for all the various needs of the modern computer, logic, fast memory, and slower low-power memory. The design of fast memory already uses parallelism in some form and is 'non-destructive read-out'. The slower memory is 'destructive read-out', which means that the data stored is locally lost when it is accessed. This again adds to the complexity of the technology, as a means for the regular restoring of data has to be devised.

The fabrication chips will obviously be intricate, and as the junction thickness is very important (being measured in atomic spacings), high quality will be imperative. As operating speeds are so high and distances between components so small the design of the computer as a whole has to take into account the finiteness of the speed of light. The technological problems are indeed great, and the chance of success should be assessed fully accepting that silicon implementation has not yet reached its zenith and its effectiveness will be extended greatly by future progress in concurrency and parallelism.

An interesting point to note with superconductor physics is that phenomena involving a single quantum are observable. A superconducting ring can capture magnetic field lines and retain them seemingly for ever. The magnetic field is quantised, and so the captured field represents an integer (not just a boolean) which can be remembered without power loss. The aim for computer innovators in the next century will be to reach the limits imposed by physics, quantum effects, the speed of light (optical devices), and atomic scales (molecular electronics).

6.4.2   Optical computers

It is probably safe to say that the possibility of the optical computer has received more attention recently than the other emerging technologies, as evidenced by recent articles in *Computers in Physics* (Mar/Apr, 1988). This may well be because laser optics is a means of communication in space, because optical fibres and optical discs are fast developing and are in the public eye, or because we all know that nothing can go faster than light and therefore no computer will go faster than an optical computer. This last argument may satisfy a politician, but we should look a little more closely. If we do, we will come to the same conclusion as with superconductivity, namely that this book will be long since out of date and out of print before the optical computer makes an impact. Nevertheless it is very clear that an understanding of parallelism, especially SIMD parallelism, will be of central importance for its ultimate success.

The basic physical phenomenon underpinning research in this field is known as 'optical bistability'. The devices used have the two stable conditions which are essential for logic manipulation. They are made from thin plates of special materials between two partially reflecting surfaces, known as Fabry-Perot plates. One example of the special material in these plates is zinc selenide ($ZnSe$), which has a pronounced non-linear refractive index in the visible range. This means that the optical density of the material changes with the intensity of light in the material, and as the optical density changes the speed of light in the material changes. The light in the plate reflects backwards and forwards between the partially reflecting surfaces, giving a transmitted beam which is the sum of many small beams. The way these beams add together depends on the velocity of light in the device. When they are all 'coherent' or 'in phase', a large intensity is transmitted, and this large intensity causes the intensity in the device itself to be large, latching the velocity of light to the special value which sustains the large transmitted intensity.

In the off state, the device transmits a beam of laser light which in itself is not intense enough to give the special value of the velocity of light. The device can then be switched on by a momentary injection of intensity, latching the velocity of light to the special value which then persists after the intensity injection subsides. To undo the latch and switch the device off some further reduction of the original beam has to be done, which is not difficult as this beam is the sum of a 'holding beam' and another beam which carries some information. All the various logical functions can be constructed with such devices.

The switching between states involves the interaction between the light intensity and the solid state material, and therefore its speed is determined not by the speed of light but by a solid state process. It is hoped that gates with a switching speed of $1\mu s$ will soon be developed, with power dissipation between 10 and 100 μW. Precisely controlled layered materials are now being fabricated by molecular beam epitaxial (or non-epitaxial) growth, giving considerable prospects for improved materials in the future. Other devices made from liquid crystals perform at these low powers, though not with such speeds, but the devices described above are the ones which give rise to the most natural parallel applications.

To achieve gates with very low power dissipation, very small laser beams are used. The fineness of these beams will be limited by diffraction and therefore the optical wavelength, but they can be so fine that thousands of independent beams can interact with a plate of (say) $1cm^2$. Production of plates with sufficient perfection over such areas is not such a thorny task as producing the myriad beams with individually controlled intensities. A single laser beam can be divided into an array of beams, a square array, a honeycomb or whatever is required, by the use of a specially prepared hologram, and we expect to see much progress in the perfection of these holograms. Thus the SIMD parallel beams can be produced, and the big challenge is to be able to control them by merging beams, a necessary step both for logic control and for simply sustaining an optical current.

The separate devices do not need any physical contacts; this is a particular attraction at a time when everyone argues that the most expensive parts of a modern computer are the connecting wires. Another attraction is that light beams can pass through the same volume of space without interacting with each other, giving an enormous flexibility for reconfiguration. The combination of advantages and disadvantages probably means that the future optical computer will be used for problems somewhat more specific than the silicon-based SIMD counterparts, and while the all-optical computer is being developed we will certainly see some of the major advances in the form of opto-electronic devices. This is surely a very exciting research field.

6.4.3   Molecular electronics

The phrase 'molecular electronics' has been coined in recent years, and there has been surprisingly strong financial support for work in this area, although the meaning of the phrase is by no means agreed upon. This is quite understandable as each research group interprets the phrase according to its own interests. What is common to all interpretations is that fabrication is to be done at the most fine level attainable. Thus it is that some research groups are trying to produce the means for controlled fabrication with linewidths down to 10nm, but we would prefer the more literal interpretation, as made by Forrest Carter, that the object is to be able to make computing elements out of molecules.

Any molecule with the correct characteristics for device fabrication must have the ability to conduct a pulse. Such molecules must then be interconnected in such a way that the interconnects (nodes) function as logic gates. The conduction of a pulse in one molecule must not interfere with a pulse elsewhere except through the nodes, and so there must be some form of

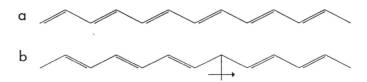

Figure 6.7: (a) Section of a trans-polyacetylene chain, $(CH)_x$. (b) As the pulse moves to the right the position of the double bond changes.

isolation. The conducting molecule and its insulation are thus very similar to living nerve cells, and therefore, as Forrest Carter points out, the brain serves as a proof of existence for a molecular electronic computer. The brain is simultaneously a parallel and a concurrent computer, and we can safely predict that developments in computer parallel and concurrent software will be vital for the success of the molecular electronic computer.

Are there any molecules which can be considered for use in such a computer? First let us consider molecules which can support an energy pulse, travelling like a soliton. Solitons, which were first observed by Scott Russell in the Union Canal in Scotland, are single wave crest pulses which move through the carrying medium with very little change in shape over a large distance. Such behaviour is possible in certain polymers, such as trans-polyacetylene $(CH)_x$ as shown in figure 6.7(a). Here there is an alternation between single and double bonds along the chain, and the pulse takes the form of a change in the bonding seen to be occurring in figure 6.7(b), as the pulse moves to the right.

Now let us see how switching may be attempted with these polymer chains. Taking the example of figure 6.8 the simplest possible node joining four sections of polymer chain, we can easily work out the possible final states of the node after a pulse has been received on any of the four channels. The rule to be applied is that no atoms in the chain (the angle points in these diagrams) may partake in more than one double bond. Thus if a pulse arrives on channel B (left diagram) it departs on channel C right diagram. Note that if the pulse arrives on channel A while the node is in the state shown by the diagram on the left then the final pulse could

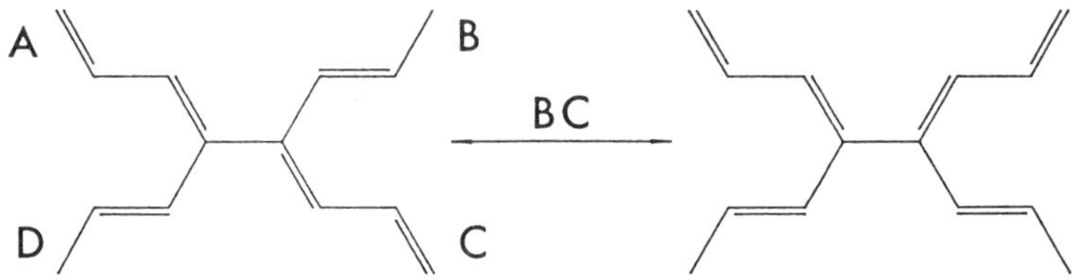

Figure 6.8: Node forming a simple soliton switch

depart on channel C or D, though C may be favoured for pulse momentum reasons. These examples are not necessarily those which will be used in future molecular electronic computers, but they are demonstrations of what might be feasible and we should therefore not discount the possibility of such a technology.

The final question to be asked here is what sort of computer could be constructed from these molecules? Parallelism and concurrency need no further argument, but will it be possible to make a computer which exactly matches some specification? Silicon chips with faults on them are usually useless, and we would expect the same to be true for superconductor devices. Many optical devices (such as spatial light modulators) play a role between the digital and the analogue, and in the latter role the possibility of there being noise is assumed. In the molecular computer we may have to plan for there being a certain level of defects in any desired interconnection, and for using the computer without the strict discipline of synchronisation time points. Such a computer is a neural computer, whose interconnect structure need not be known exactly and which can be used after a modicum of teaching. The ability of neural networks to function depends very much on the total number of neurons, and the possibility of making machines of a very high device density and low power consumption is extremely exciting. Put neural networks and molecular electronics with optical devices, high temperature superconductivity and parallel computation and no funding source can possibly resist. Perhaps there will be some advances quicker than we would think!

References

GHEEWALA *Proc. IEEE*, 70, 1982, pp 26-34.

FORREST CARTER *Nonlinear Electrodynamics in Biological Systems*, eds. Adey & Lawrence, Plenum, 1984, pp 243-273.

Index

Computing Books from Chartwell-Bratt

GENERAL COMPUTING BOOKS

Compiler Physiology for Beginners, M Farmer, 279pp, ISBN 0-86238-064-2
Dictionary of Computer and Information Technology, D Lynch, 225 pages, ISBN 0-86238-128-2
File Structure and Design, M Cunningham, 211pp, ISBN 0-86238-065-0
Information Technology Dictionary of Acronyms and Abbreviations, D Lynch, 270pp, ISBN 0-86238-153-3
The IBM Personal Computer with BASIC and PC-DOS, B Kynning, 320pp, ISBN 0-86238-080-4

PROGRAMMING LANGUAGES

An Intro to LISP, P Smith, 130pp, ISBN 0-86238-187-8
An Intro to OCCAM 2 Programming, Bowler, *et al,* 109pp, ISBN 0-86238-137-1
Cobol for Mainframe and Micro: 2nd Ed, D Watson, 177pp, ISBN 0-86238-211-4
Comparative Languages: 2nd Ed, J R Malone, 125pp, ISBN 0-86238-123-1'
Fortran 77 for Non-Scientists, P Adman, 109pp, ISBN 0-86238-074-X
Fortran 77 Solutions to Non-Scientific Problems, P Adman, 150pp, ISBN 0-86238-087-1
Fortran Lectures at Oxford, F Pettit, 135pp, ISBN 0-86238-122-3
LISP: From Foundations to Applications, G Doukidis *et al,* 228pp, ISBN 0-86238-191-6
Prolog versus You, A-L Johansson, 296pp, ISBN 0-86238-174-6
Simula Begin, G M Birtwistle *et al,* 391pp, ISBN 0-86238-009-X
The Intensive C Course, M Farmer, 167pp, ISBN 0-86238-114-2
The Intensive Pascal Course, M Farmer, 111pp, ISBN 0-86238-063-4

ASSEMBLY LANGUAGE PROGRAMMING

Coding the 68000, N Hellawell, 214pp, ISBN 0-86238-180-0
Computer Organisation and Assembly Language Programming, L Ohlsson & P Stenstrom, 128pp, ISBN 0-86238-129-0
What is machine code and what can you do with it? N Hellawell, 104pp, ISBN 0-86238-132-0

PROGRAMMING TECHNIQUES

Discrete-events simulations models in PASCAL/MT+ on a microcomputer, L P Jennergren, 135pp, ISBN 0-86238-053-7
Information and Coding, J A Llewellyn, 152pp, ISBN 0-86238-099-5
JSP - A Practical Method of Program Design: 2nd Ed, L Ingevaldsson, 204pp, ISBN 0-86238-107-X
JSD - Method for System Development, L Ingevaldsson, 248pp, ISBN 0-86238-103-7

Programming for Beginners: the structured way, D Bell & P Scott, 178pp, ISBN 0-86238-130-4

Software Engineering for Students, M Coleman & S Pratt, 195pp, ISBN 0-86238-115-0

Software Taming with Dimensional Design, M Coleman & S Pratt, 164pp, ISBN 0-86238-142-8

Systems Programming with JSP, B Sanden, 186pp, ISBN 0-86238-054-5

MATHEMATICS AND COMPUTING

Fourier Transforms in Action, F Pettit, 133pp, ISBN 0-86238-088-X

Generalised Coordinates, L G Chambers, 90pp, ISBN 0-86238-079-0

Linear Programming: A Computational Approach: 2nd Ed, K K Lau, 150pp, ISBN 0-86238-182-7

Statistics and Operations Research, I Schagen, 300pp, ISBN 0-86238-077-4

Teaching of Modern Engineering Mathematics, L Rade (ed), 225pp, ISBN 0-86238-173-8

Teaching of Statistics in the Computer Age, L Rade (ed), 248pp, ISBN 0-86238-090-1

The Essentials of Numerical Computation, M Bartholomew-Biggs, 241pp, ISBN 0-86238-029-4

DATABASES AND MODELLING

Computer Systems Modelling & Development, D Cornwell, 200pp, ISBN 0-86238-220-3

Database Analysis and Design, H Robinson, 378pp, ISBN 0-86238-018-9

Databases and Database Systems, E Oxborrow, 256pp, ISBN 0-86238-091-X

Data Bases and Data Models, B Sundgren, 134pp, ISBN 0-86238-031-6

Text Retrieval and Document Databases, J Ashford/P Willett, 125pp, ISBN 0-86238-204-1

Information Modelling, J Bubenko (ed), 687pp, ISBN 0-86238-006-5

UNIX

An Intro to the Unix Operating System, C Duffy, 152p, ISBN 0-86238-143-6

Operating Systems through Unix, G Emery, 96pp, ISBN 0-86238-086-3

SYSTEMS ANALYSIS AND DEVELOPMENT

Systems Analysis and Development: 3rd Ed, P Layzell & P Loucopoulos, 272pp, ISBN 0-86238-215-7

SYSTEMS DESIGN

Computer Systems: Where Hardware meets Software, C Machin, 200pp, ISBN 0-86238-075-8

Distributed Applications and Online Dialogues: a design method for application systems, A Rasmussen, 271pp, ISBN 0-86238-105-3

Microcomputer Systems: hardware and software, J Tierney, 168pp, ISBN 0-86238-218-1

SSADM Techniques, M Leijk, *et al*, 350pp, ISBN 0-86238-224-6

HARDWARE

Computers from First Principles, M Brown, 128pp, ISBN 0-86238-027-8
Fundamentals of Microprocessor Systems, P Witting, 525pp,
ISBN 0-86238-030-8

ELECTRICAL & ELECTRONIC ENGINEERING

Analogue and Digital Signal Processing and Coding, P M Grant, *et al*,
450pp, ISBN 0-86238-206-8
Handbook of Electronics, J de Sousa Pires, 800pp, ISBN 0-86238-061-8

NETWORKS

Communication Network Protocols: 2nd Ed, B Marsden, 345pp,
ISBN 0-86238-106-1
Computer Networks: Fundamentals and Practice, M D Bacon *et al*, 109pp,
ISBN 0-86238-028-6
Datacommunication: Data Networks, Protocols and Design, L Ewald &
E Westman, 343pp, ISBN 0-86238-092-8
Data Networks 1, Ericsson & Televerket, ISBN 0-86238-193-2
Telecommunications: Telephone Networks 1, Ericsson & Televerket, 147pp,
ISBN 0-86238-093-6
Telecommunications: Telephone Networks 2, Ericsson & Televerket, 176pp,
ISBN 0-86238-113-4

GRAPHICS

An Introductory Course in Computer Graphics, R Kingslake, 146pp,
ISBN 0-86238-073-1
Techniques of Interactive Computer Graphics, A Boyd, 242pp,
ISBN 0-86238-024-3
Two-dimensional Computer Graphics, S Laflin, 85pp, ISBN 0-86238-127-4

APPLICATIONS

Computers in Health and Fitness, J Abas, 106pp, ISBN 0-86238-155-X
Developing Expert Systems, G Doukidis, E Whitley, ISBN 0-86238-196-7
Expert Systems Introduced, D Daly, 180pp, ISBN 0-86238-185-1
Handbook of Finite Element Software, J Mackerle & B Fredriksson, approx
1000pp, ISBN 0-86238-135-5
Inside Data Processing: computers and their effective use in business,
A deWatteville, 150pp, ISBN 0-86238-181-9
Proceedings of the Third Scandinavian Conference on Image Analysis,
P Johansen & P Becker (eds) 426pp, ISBN 0-86238-039-1
Programmable Control Systems, G Johannesson, 136pp, ISBN 0-86238-046-4
Project Skills Handbook, S Rogerson, approx 100pp, ISBN 0-86238-146-0
Risk and Reliability Appraisal on Microcomputers, G Singh, + G Kiangi,

142pp, ISBN 0-86238-159-2
Statistics with Lotus 1-2-3, M Lee & J Soper, 207pp, ISBN 0-86238-131-2

HCI

Human/Computer Interaction: from voltage to knowledge, J Kirakowski, 250pp, ISBN 0-86238-179-7
Information Ergonomics, T Ivegard, 228pp, ISBN 0-86238-032-4
Computer Display Designer's Handbook, E Wagner, approx 300pp, ISBN 0-86238-171-1

INFORMATION AND SOCIETY

Access to Government Records: International Perspectives and Trends, T Riley, 112pp, ISBN 0-86238-119-3
CAL/CBT - the great debate, D Marshall, 300pp, ISBN 0-86238-144-4
Economic and Trade-Related Aspects of Transborder Dataflow, R Wellington-Brown, 93pp, ISBN 0-86238-110-X
Information Technology and a New International Order, J Becker, 141pp, ISBN 0-86238-043-X
People or Computers: 3 ways of looking at information systems, M Nurminen, 1218pp, ISBN 0-86238-184-3
Transnational Data Flows in the Information Age, C Hamelink, 115pp, ISBN 0-86238-042-1

MATHS & SCIENCE HANDBOOKS

Alpha Maths Handbook, L Rade, 199pp, ISBN 0-86238-036-7
Beta Maths Handbook, L Rade, 425pp, ISBN 0-86238-140-1
Nuclear Analytical Chemistry, D Brune *et al,* 557pp, ISBN 0-86238-047-2
Physics Handbook, C Nordling & J Osterman, 430pp, ISBN 0-86238-037-5
The V-Belt Handbook, H Palmgren, 287pp, ISBN 0-86238-111-8

Chartwell-Bratt specialise in excellent books at affordable prices.

For further details contact your local bookshop, or ring Chartwell-Bratt direct on **01-467 1956**(Access/Visa welcome.)

Ring or write for our *free* catalogue.

Chartwell-Bratt (Publishing & Training) Ltd, Old Orchard, Bickley Road, Bromley, Kent, BR1 2NE, United Kingdom.
Tel 01-467 1956, Fax 01-467 1754, Telecom Gold 84:KJM001, Telex 9312100451(CB)

Dictionary of Computer and Information Technology Terms

BY DON LYNCH

Sets out in a concise and easily understood manner brief explanations of over 2500 of the most common words, terms, jargon, acronyms, abbreviations and codes associated with information technology. The text provides a comprehensive and non-technical reference source and guide for users of computer and information technology in education and business. It makes the terminology and jargon of computer and information science readily understandable and available to the non-expert - at a very affordable price.

225 pages, ISBN 0-86238-128-2

CURRENT PRICE £5.95 (confirm details before ordering)

Available from your local bookshop, or direct from
Chartwell-Bratt, Old Orchard, Bickley Road, Bromley, Kent, BR1 2NE, UK. Tel 01-467 1956, Fax 01-467 1754